River Teeth Literary Nonfiction Prize

SERIES EDITORS:
Daniel Lehman, *Ashland University*
Joe Mackall, *Ashland University*

The River Teeth Literary Nonfiction Prize is
awarded to the best work of literary nonfiction
submitted to the annual contest sponsored by
River Teeth: A Journal of Nonfiction Narrative.

THE ENDERS HOTEL

A MEMOIR

BRANDON R. SCHRAND

UNIVERSITY OF NEBRASKA PRESS • LINCOLN AND LONDON

Portions of chapters 3, 10, 13,
and the epilogue originally
appeared as "The Enders Hotel"
in *Green Mountains Review*
19, no. 2 (Fall/Winter 2006):
132–44.
A slightly different version of
chapter 17 originally appeared
as "Collusion" in *Drunken Boat*,
no. 9 (2007), http://www
.drunkenboat.com/.

Library of Congress
Cataloging-in-Publication Data
Schrand, Brandon R.
The Enders Hotel: a memoir /
Brandon R. Schrand.
p.   cm. — (River teeth literary
nonfiction prize)
ISBN 978-0-8032-1769-0
(paper: alk. paper)
1. Schrand, Brandon R.—
Childhood and youth.
2. Schrand, Brandon R.—
Family.   3. Soda Springs
(Idaho)—Biography.   4. Enders
Hotel (Soda Springs, Idaho)
5. Hotelkeepers—Idaho—Soda
Springs—Biography.   6. Soda
Springs (Idaho)—Social life and
customs—20th century. I. Title.
F754.S6S37   2008
979.6'45—dc22
2007034364

Set in Stone Serif
by Bob Reitz.
Designed by
R. W. Boeche.

Acknowledgments

I am thankful first and foremost to my wife and children for their undying support and love. Thanks beyond my most immediate family go to the legions of supporters who helped make this book a reality. In particular, I am deeply indebted to my mother, Karen Schrand, and my grandmother Beth Beus for the hundreds of phone calls that helped clarify the story I was trying to tell. And to my father, Bud Schrand, who always supported my need to tell this story.

I am thankful, too, to Kim Barnes, Mary Clearman Blew, and Rodney Frey for their enduring friendship as well as their close and careful suggestions offered in varying stages of the manuscript. My longtime friend Michael Donovan offered his shrewd and right-minded advice in nearly every phase of the book. Timothy Schaffert's comments and suggestions in a late stage of revision were especially invaluable. To Jeff Jones, Ben George, Nate Lowe, and Bryan Fry—the brotherhood who never doubted—I offer my gratitude.

For their enthusiasm and willingness to help at every turn, I thank the following: Rex and Brent Maughan, who rescued the

Enders Hotel, and for their generosity and openness while I was researching this book; Cindy Erickson and the folks at the Soda Springs Public Library for their unfailing kindness and love of books; and the staff at the Caribou County Courthouse for un-earthing much-needed documents.

I must thank Joe Mackall and everyone at *River Teeth* for believing in this story so thoroughly, and for bringing it to light. Finally, it has been a real pleasure to work with Ladette Randolph, Margie Rine, and Ann Baker at the University of Nebraska Press.

1. Restless Men

On a rain-soaked afternoon in August of 1975 my mother took her shift behind the counter in the bar of the Enders Hotel. It would have been an ordinary afternoon in Soda Springs, Idaho, if not for the sudden downpour in that stretch of summer's furnace-breath. The rains drove farmers into the dank hollows of their Quonset huts that hugged the rocky landscape. And they sent, too, the ore-mine roughnecks scampering for cover. Some jobs shut down all together. Irrigation lines stopped surging their rainbow arc of canal water over the season's last run of alfalfa. But because it is high desert country, the rains passed, as they always do, and the clouds cleared as evening dragged across the basalt flows and barley fields, brooming the sky of its light.

Hours later, a man named Larry who was staying in one of the hotel rooms upstairs, shot and killed his best friend, Charlie—point blank—on our barroom floor. It was an accident, a drunken misunderstanding, as so many of these things are.

For first-degree murder, Larry was given a life sentence and sent to the Idaho State Penitentiary. He was admitted only a couple of months after my father, Jerry Imeson, a man I would never meet, had been released from the same prison for knocking over a pharmacy.

Larry was thirty. Charlie was thirty-three, and my father twenty-three.

All these restless men.

My family had not owned the Enders Hotel but six months before that man's blood soaked the carpet. And although his would be the only murder to occur under that ceiling while we owned the place, he wouldn't be the only one to die there, or who would otherwise vanish.

2. Reconstruction

It was a rough patch for my mother. With her ex-lover (my father) recently paroled and out of the picture, she married a sandy-haired red-faced itinerant welder, a roughneck named Kent. But that wouldn't last and they would divorce soon after. He was violent when he drank and he drank often. It is the oldest of stories. I have a singular memory of Kent burning me with a cigarette. I don't think he did it on purpose. He was sitting in our kitchen with his arm draped over the back of the chair, cigarette between two fingers. In my mind's eye, he looks like James Dean. T-shirt and jeans and leather boots. I was shirtless when I bumped into the cigarette, or it bumped into me, and it burned my chest. It's either a memory or a dream I had once. But it's always been there and whenever I hear his name I think of that orange ember hot on my skin.

A few years after their divorce, my mother would get a phone call telling her that Kent had been killed. He was drunk. It was a single-car accident on a button-hook turn along some Idaho highway. "Well," she had said. "Thank God for that."

3

During much of that period—and earlier, before the Enders Hotel—I lived with my grandparents in their green clapboard ranch house east of town while my mother tried with varying degrees of success to get on her feet. The house had a long and wide wooden porch that peered off into a grove of crab apple trees, and beyond those, a flickering stand of aspens, and farther still, miles of open barley fields. A 1940s black Mercury sat on its rusted rims beneath the trees and was overgrown with sweet peas. Worm-holed crab apples dropped to the black hood in percussive thuds. The windows were long gone and springs jutted through the boxy seats. The car looked like an insect carcass and I loved it intensely. I would spend hours in that car with my cousins Jade and Angel who lived across the dooryard in the yellow clapboard. This was the Beus Ranch, a hundred-year-old operation of sheep and barley that grew to some six thousand acres. If the Enders Hotel, Bar, and Café comprised one half of our family legacy and inheritance—if there ever was such a thing—the Beus ranch comprised the other half.

My grandmother often recalls my "episodes" from that time. "You used to beat your head against the walls," she always says. "You were so damned frustrated." The story is always the same. "So your grandpa got down one day and hit *his* head against the wall. You thought that was the funniest thing you'd ever seen, and you never did it again."

When my grandparents decided to buy the Enders Hotel, they leased the ranch to my uncle—Jade and Angel's father—and moved into town where they unloaded their belongings in a spacious, skylit apartment on the ground floor. It was a high-ceilinged place with arched doorways, crystal doorknobs, and featured an enormous set of built-in cedarwood bookshelves with leaded glass. Initially, when my mother couldn't arrange for another sitter, my grandparents tended me in this apartment. Years later it would become my home.

Not long after the shooting in the bar, my mother met Bud Schrand, a recently divorced dark-skinned electrician with long jet-black hair who wore leather wrist bands and paisley shirts. An out-of-towner, Bud drove a purple 1971 Dodge Charger and their first dates were spent drag racing other roughnecks up and down the streets of Soda Springs and on the outlaying farm roads. Later he would total the Charger (without my mother) and buy a 1974 Plymouth Roadrunner—a white one with a red racing stripe. Bud, who had two daughters of his own who lived elsewhere, moved in with us, and we lived in Soda Springs for a few months before moving fifty-some miles west to Pocatello. I remember fragments from that place. A one-room apartment at the end of a junked-out alley. Ants littered the speckled bathroom floor. I slept on the couch and shredded my T-shirts while I slept. I ripped each one so that when I woke, my fingers were sore, and I wore only white ribbons.

It wasn't long before we aimed the Roadrunner for the southeastern desert of West Richland, Washington. We had become job seekers. Bud hired on at the Hanford Nuclear Reactor site. There we moved into a white clapboard house that stood at the edge of a brushy field a quarter mile from the sandy banks of the Columbia River. That was 1976 when he and my mother were talking about marriage. I was four. I remember the desert heat and the white paint that flecked off the clapboard like blistered skin, a hush of fallout that speckled my fingertips when I touched it in the shadow of the eaves.

Those years in Washington are remembered for their extremes. We were a family. We went on vacations. We went camping. We ate together every night. My mother cooked. I helped wash the dishes. But there was the drinking. The slammed doors. The yelling and all the upset that occurs along that kind of alcoholic fault line. Bud had been thrown in jail for drunk driving, but my mother lucked out. Instead of getting stopped by police, she crashed our green pickup into the side of an iron bridge. No one was hurt, but when she lurched the truck into the driveway, the passenger fender was crushed and one headlight dangled out like an eye popped from its socket.

Because we were job seekers, we endured the perpetual ebb and flow of work—the overtime followed, always, by the lay-offs, the shut-downs, the walkouts. This cyclic pattern first flung us into the desert near Hanford, only to send us back to the Enders Hotel in Soda Springs (during a walk-off); once again back to Hanford (when a deal was brokered).

Then one day Bud came home from Hanford and said the electrical workers and others were going on strike—again. "Could be a sixty-day walkout. Could be a ninety-day walkout. Just depends." The workers organized the strike in response to widespread corruption that had then recently come to light. My mother spent hours on the phone with my grandmother. In her housecoat, on our golden couches, wreathed in cigarette smoke. I was crouched on the floor playing with dozens of green plastic army men and would look up at her every now and again and try to guess what it was she was talking about by weighing the seriousness of her tone. Then one morning she hung up, looked at me, and said, "So, Brandon, how would you like to stay with Grandma and Grandpa for awhile?"

As it turned out, the walkout could not have come at a better time. Shortly after we moved to Washington, my grandparents received an offer they initially dismissed, but later accepted. The United States Forest Service wanted to lease the Enders Building for their Youth Conservation Corps (YCC) for one year. That year, my grandparents thought, would give them some time to seek treatment for my grandfather's emphysema with which he had been recently diagnosed. So in 1978, three years after buying it, three years after a man lost his life on their barroom floor, they shut down the entire operation and turned it over to the YCC. Busloads of gangly troubled youths arrived in Soda Springs, luggage in tow, and filed into the Enders Building. In twelve months they had nearly destroyed the place. They painted rooms and hallways in psychedelic hues of orange and bright green, flowers and mushrooms and peace signs. Someone painted one room on the third story in a black and white swirl that caused momentary vertigo when you stood in its vortex. Another room featured a sign that read, THE GETTING LOADED ZONE. But the destruction exceeded cosmetics. Busted chairs cluttered hallways. Wiring panels were gutted, the plumbing ransacked, carpet scalped from its floor. They slashed mattresses, smashed mirrors, shattered china, and defaced paintings. The building looked ship-wrecked.

A year later, in the final months of 1979, when my grandparents walked in the abandoned building on a bright afternoon and pushed through the lobby doors, it was as though part of them had been killed in the process. My grandmother paled. My grandfather kicked a clump of lath across the floor. Their complaints fell on unsympathetic ears at the local level of the Forest Service, but within weeks, my grandfather gave a tour to a Forest Service director at the state level. The director's mouth fell agape when he saw the damage. "We'll make it right," the director kept saying.

"I know you will," my grandfather said. "I know you will."

And so it was decided that during the walkout, we would pack a few things, lock up the house in Washington (our neighbors, the landlords, would watch over it), and go back to Soda Springs, to the Enders Hotel, and help in the recovery. We crossed Oregon's Blue Mountains in our Plymouth Roadrunner loaded down with suitcases. This was early summer 1980. My mother sat in front, a pile of nerves, snapping her gum, and flicking cigarette ashes out the window. If Dad was a confident driver (and at times overconfident, even menacing), my mother was neurotic, solicitous, certain our traffic deaths were imminent, particularly through high passes like those in the Blue Mountains. Never mind that shafts of sunlight washed through the forest's canopy, and that the road was dry, or that if we rolled down the window we could smell the rich scent of piney earth. My mother feared travel in any conditions. "Buddy, slow down," she said. "Slow. Down."

"Going too slow causes more wrecks than going too fast, Karen," he said.

Eventually we arrived safely at the Enders Hotel where my mother and dad took a small apartment on the ground floor that had an outer entrance from the alley, and another that opened into the lobby. It was situated between my grandparents' apartment and the Enders Bar, and its living room transformed into a bedroom by dropping the Murphy bed down from behind a set of closet doors. A tiny kitchen and bathroom flanked either side of the living room. Because of its impossible size, I would stay in my grandparents' spacious apartment next door.

That first day back I followed my grandfather up to the third story to retrieve my rollaway bed. He carried a jangling set of keys that retracted on a chain to a spool clipped to his belt. A place with so many doors required many keys. On the third floor, we turned down the dimly lit hallway, stopped before a room, and my grandfather pulled a key from the set and opened the door. The room was unfinished and housed a half dozen rollaway beds, one of which was reclined. "Hop on," he said.

I lay down across the middle of the bed with my arms and feet barely dangling over the edges. He folded up the bed with me in it, locked it in place with a bar at the top, so that I was sandwiched in the bed with my head sticking out one side and my toes out the other. Then he started wheeling me down the hallway on the bed's casters. I felt pinched but comfortable. As he eased the bed down four flights of stairs, I squealed and pretended to be afraid that he might let go and the bed and I would go bouncing down flight after flight of stairs. After he rolled me into the apartment and unfastened the lock-bar at the top of the bed, my grandmother stepped in to see me. The café was closing, she said, and then she would be right over. "Your mom will be over soon."

My grandmother positioned the bed directly beneath an enormous skylight into which I stared. Beyond the apartment's doors I could hear the building breathe and move, shift and settle. Cackling people from the bar who would stumble into the lobby to use the pay phone. The jukebox, and the rumbling release of billiard balls for a new game. Then a lull. After my mother came over to say goodnight, she shut off the light and I turned on my side shoving my arm beneath my pillow. The glass in the arched French doors that led from my grandparents' apartment into the lobby was opaque, so all I could see was a kaleidoscope of colors and shadows of movement. I rolled to my back, glad to be there, and looked up. Slowly I drifted off to sleep with the songs of this new place floating on my dreams.

3. A Storied History

My mother helped in the café which was then in an operable state, while Dad commuted to a job he had found in Pocatello, some fifty miles to the west. After his twelve-hour shifts and on weekends, he worked around the hotel rewiring brass lamps, attending to leaking pipes, or testing breaker and fuse boxes. There was much to do. My grandparents hired friends or those short on cash to help, too. Still, others, those who owed them money, say, showed up as well. It wasn't strange at all for me to run down one of the upstairs hallways and find someone I didn't know hauling five-gallon buckets of lathe to the fire escape where they were lowered rope-wise to the ground. Men and women alike came and went. Some vacuumed up white Sheetrock dust from green carpet while others groaned over pipe wrenches in bathrooms. And at the end of any given day, I would see a man take a sheaf of bills from my grandfather, thank him earnestly, and vanish into the smoky depths of the bar. And as often as not, I would never see that particular man again. But another would take his place. A revolving cast of broken men.

The work varied as much as the workers who did it. Walls needed a face-lift which came in the way of wallpaper with designs often more flowery than the psychedelic paint it covered. Carpet was rolled out in the hallways scenting the air with a chemical perfume of newness. Men lowered the ceilings, hung new light fixtures, installed showers in the community bathrooms where claw-footed tubs once stood. Others tarred the roof, sealing fissures and leaks, and filled walls with thick yellow fiberglass insulation. New mattresses and rollaway beds arrived on semi-trucks. Old paintings were dusted off and displayed in the café, the new dining room (where the bar had once been), and the lobby.

But the majority of the work was done by my grandparents and my mother and dad, and them alone. You couldn't count on the others.

For me, a scrawny asthmatic kid with a runny nose, nothing could have been easier, simpler, or more thrilling than being back. To run all the staircases and hallways in such a place and to eat every meal in a café was nothing short of paradise. The long yellow lunch counter in the café was L-shaped and looked like sunshine. And for every meal I would sit at a different barstool making myself at home.

The very building itself struck a deep sense of awe and wonderment in me. The Enders Hotel was a brick mammoth that heaved its three-story shadow over South Main in downtown Soda Springs, standing, essentially, as the town's center. It keeps a storied history, one that begins with an idea hatched between two German immigrant brothers, William and Theodore Enders, suited men who arrived in Soda Springs in 1882 to start a sheep ranch. Eager and entrepreneurial, the brothers worked quickly to establish themselves in the burgeoning western town. They bought some property twenty miles north of town in the grassy Enoch Valley, and went to work on their ranch. Thirty-four years later, during a commercial boom in Soda Springs, the brothers started talking about building a hotel. It is easy enough to imagine. The men, each in their fifties, would have stood on Theodore's ranch house porch, coffee cups in hand, surveying the grasslands that swept away for miles into the sky, mulling over the idea: a hotel. Yes, a hotel. Right downtown.

It was 1916 and saloons went up almost overnight. By that time, the *Chieftain*, the town's first newspaper, was in full swing. A dancehall and opera house bumped on Saturday nights. Everything followed. Here a brothel, there a jail. It was a fine town. If you had two bits and a Friday night you could do worse than to give this town a run. And that was exactly what William and Theodore intended to do.

Using their ranch as collateral, the Enders brothers approached Dr. Ellis Kackley (known locally for treating members of Butch Cassidy's gang for gunshot wounds) for sixteen thousand dollars to cover the rest of the building costs. They would spare no expense. Construction on the Enders Hotel was completed by 1919 and the hotel came to define, in many ways, the settlement that tried to shrug off its rugged, mining town image for a statelier, more refined presence. The new image, though, wasn't so much a lie as a short-lived promise.

Years later I would learn that my own family's connection to the Enders Hotel began in those early days when the bricks were still newly mortared, freshly hauled from a foundry in Utah. Even before the hotel's completion in 1919, Idaho had passed its own prohibition law giving men like my great-grandfather Albert Beus incentive to bootleg. Albert's contraband, which was funneled through a drugstore then located in the south bay of the Enders, was sold under the auspices of medicinal tonics and elixirs.

Booze moved in and out of the Enders building and cash moved in and out of wallets and off of ledgers as though it had never been there. Businessmen, teachers, farmers, miners, and drifters alike— all of them bound in their common penchant for drink—passed through the doors of that place. It was the center of town, the epicenter of everything for those people living on the western fringe of a social swell, of Fitzgerald's Jazz Age.

The basement of the building—itself occupying the space of half a downtown block—served as a boomtown speakeasy. Stories of card games, cash-backed tables, blue smoke, prostitutes from Ogden, Utah, and whiskey fights were told through the generations surviving the suited men and flapper women who lived them.

When I cast back to the dream of that place and that time, long before I was born, this is what I hear: rambling piano keys that knock out bouncing ragtime jigs. I hear Benny Goodman and his cleaned-up, formulaic incantations of New Orleans jazz. I want to hear Joe "King" Oliver's Creole Band and Louis Armstrong, but I don't know whether their sounds had yet fingered their way into the sagging taverns and plank-board brothels of sagebrush country. I want to believe they had. And if they hadn't then I want to believe that in my dream I could walk to the railroad tracks, crouch, and put an ear to the rails. I want to believe that if I listened carefully I could hear the walking bass notes and trumpeting blues songs from a Kansas City bar that bounced under city lights, two thousand miles away.

And in that dream this is what I see: smoke and dancing, cash and liquor, the rewarding glimpse of a woman's thigh, green tables under soiled lighting. And I see my great-grandfather, Albert, playing pinochle, winning some hands, losing others. Glad-handing police officers. Buying a round. Good times. Promises, promises.

4. A Traceable Past

School approached but the walkout was still in effect. Three or four times a week Dad would call the Union Hall in Washington to get updated on the state of things. He would talk into the phone with a pen and notepad in hand and nod quietly. He was an obsessive note-taker, a diagrammer, a list-maker, a cartographer of dailiness. He would ask questions and tell the person on the phone, "Hang on a second, pard. Let me get this down." He was meticulous with dates and numbers. He was a man made of details. His shirt pockets were always tined with pens, pencils, and small screwdrivers. And he always, always, carried a small notebook. His calls to the Union Hall had a singular purpose and urgency to them: to see if a deal had been brokered between the workers and the "higher-ups," as he termed them. A deal would mean we would go back. But going back to Washington was the last thing I wanted to do. Whenever my mother broached the subject, I would offer my firm response: "I want to stay here forever."

I wanted to stay because of the hotel but also because I adored my grandparents. Lynn Beus was not my biological grandfather—an unspoken truth in a family patterned more on divorce than on marital longevity—but he was my grandfather just the same, and his family, including his bootlegging father, Albert, was mine, even if genetics said otherwise. Besides, I had no recollection of my biological grandfather, George Moyer, and had only a vague understanding that he, like my own father, was out there somewhere in the world. Perhaps that is why I had made it my goal to know as much as I could about Lynn and the Beus family: because he was there. By the time I was eleven, I had become something of an expert on the Beus genealogy, taking what I knew from a mammoth-sized hard-back book, *Whence & Whither*, the official family history. I took immense pride in memorizing minutia such as birthdates of my grandfather's third cousins or the ranks of the Beus men who had been gunned down in the trenches of World War II.

But when it came to my biological father, Jerry Imeson, I had no such book, no traceable history, no index, no photographs, no pedigree charts. (Years would pass before I thought to ask about Bud's family history.) All I possessed was a polished scrap of conversation my mother had passed on to me whenever I asked. And it was the same response every time as if it had been recorded and looped back to me: "He was a good man, Brandon. You need to know that. He never laid a hand on me. You should know that too. And he adored you. It was just one of those things, though, that wasn't going to work out."

"What did he do?" I asked once. "Like for a living?"

"He was a painter," my mother said.

My eyes widened. An artist, I thought.

"He painted houses."

"Oh," I said, my voice flattening.

"And when he broke his leg skiing, he couldn't work, and that is when I made the decision that I—that we—had to move on."

"Oh."

That was the sum total of what I knew about Jerry Imeson. I did not know what he looked like or that he had been to prison for robbing a drugstore. I knew nothing. So without the written stories, I had taken to creating my own tales. In one story, I placed him in the jungles of Vietnam as a POW. That was a story I could take to school, one I could offer when people noticed my step-dad's dark skin and compared it to my own fair complexion. In another story, the one I told myself before I drifted off to sleep at night, Jerry shows up as a guest in our hotel and then decides to live with us. All of us. One big happy family under all that ceiling. Over time, it had become more of a promise than a story. Soon, I half-believed it.

I knew enough about my biological grandfather, George, that I didn't feel as compelled to invent stories about him. I had seen his picture. I had heard the tales from my mother. The box-jawed cowboy. The decorated war hero. The sheriff in Jackson Hole, Wyoming. The singing Westerner who seemed poised to walk off the page of a dime novel. It was enough to paint a picture and that seemed to satisfy my curiosity for the time being. My grand-mother, on the other hand, never talked about her ex-husband. For her, there was simply nothing to discuss. The end of the story was the whole story, and that was that.

But the man I considered my real grandfather—Lynn Beus—was alive and present and could tell me his own stories. A rancher all his life, he embodied the best and worst of small town Idaho culture. He was generous, often to a fault. He had an engineer's mind that was inventive, resourceful, and pragmatic. Once, when the harvest season was stalled by relentless rains, he welded a coal furnace and large system of exhaust fans on a combine harvester, improvising a contraption that would blow-dry his grain as he cut it. Unbelievably, incredibly, it worked. But he was also obstinate, brazen in his will. He was a gambler who bought a small craps table onto which he threw dice in the afternoons before his naps, not-ing the numbers of each toss in a notebook that would map the laws of probability. He was a voracious reader. A believer in natural medicine. An Armageddonist. A libertarian, who, upon hearing paranoid chatter about the government's plans to repeal the Second Amendment, stockpiled weapons and munitions in the hotel basement. Something of an Edgar Cayce and Nostradamus enthusiast, he often talked about extrasensory perception and the great quake that would sink California. A recovering alcoholic, he was spiritual but not religious. In his later years, he relinquished the hunting life, but found solace in the pulse of casting a fly-line on open water. He was a forward-thinker who, for instance, defended organic farming before it earned its chic name. His charm and persuasiveness could, with ease, turn into manipulation with nary a sign. And he could be maddeningly backwards (to his mind men were superior to women).

He called me The Brat, and I worshipped him.

My grandmother was petite and wore glasses like my mother, but her hair was cut short like a boy's. Years of smoking menthols had obliterated her sense of smell and added a shot of gravel to her voice. When she answered the phone, strangers would often mistake her for a man. Like her husband, grandmother read constantly, a habit passed on to my mother, and eventually on to me. We were a family of very little education (most lucky to graduate high school), but what we lacked in degrees we made up for in bulk reading. Grandmother claims to this day that she was the only student to have read every book in their library by the time she graduated high school. The library would have been small, but her fascination with stories, I think, speaks for itself. I imagine her then while a war raged on overseas—a war that would claim her brother—and how she would have fingered a row of books, stopping on the next unfamiliar title. A new story that promised a new escape.

She was legendary in Soda Springs in the way some people are legendary in small towns. Her name—Beth Beus—resonated wherever it was spoken. Farmers would wink at hearing her name and dole out one of several stock lines like "Hard worker," or "She's worn out more work boots than most men I know." Whenever these comments got back to her, my grandmother stayed true to the code of such things by laughing first and then by disarming the compliment: "Oh, horseshit," she'd say. But beneath the self-deprecation there was always a sense of pride there because it was true, and I admired her for her reputation.

She drove combines, grain trucks, learned how to weld, milk cattle, run a bunkhouse, dock lambs, fix leaking pipes, frame a wall, whatever task was set before her. Standing only five feet tall, she taught my uncle how to play basketball at night down at the Quonset hut on the ranch under the yellow shroud of a dooryard light. Her drinking, of course, threatened to erode her will and her legacy, but in the end it was her will itself that squelched that lingering thirst.

I was happy then, and everything felt good. Night would stay night. Day would stay day. Everything was secure. In the café I loved the black and red tiled floor that to me looked like a large checker board. And I loved how pork chops or eggs spattered on the grill in the kitchen. I would sit at a table and kick my feet, nicking the floor now and again, drinking a cold grape soda through a long straw. I loved how the place smelled of smoke and coffee and grilled sandwiches, and how it was filled with people and sunlight, and how the people knew my name as if they had always known me. I liked that country music crooned from the green jukebox in the corner, and how everyone in the café knew each other and they were here because of my family. I had become part of this place.

5. Patterns

Those days spilled forth easily. At lunch my grandfather worked the cash register, and in the afternoons he punched in numbers on his ten-key calculator issuing white ribbons of accounting that looped from the small machine and snaked across his desk. Meanwhile my grandmother ran the kitchen, preparing the daily specials, and could be found whisking a roux in a large steaming pot. My mother rolled out plats of pie dough, while cooks snapped meal tickets from the silvery spindle in the order window. It was a rhythm I had come to trust in just a matter of weeks.

Then one day, a pattern from our past emerged and threatened to unravel that rhythm. I was in the café perched at the yellow lunch counter sucking down a suicide—a soda comprised of every flavor from the fountain—when I heard a commotion from the lobby. I threw my gaze to the door and saw my mother—decked in a T-shirt and bell-bottom jeans—stumbling into the café. I recognized the boozy staggered gait, the fumbling, the flushed face, and glazed eyes. Her purse sliding from her shoulder. It was a spectacle I had grown used to in Washington. Everyone in the café—customers, waitresses, the cooks and dishwasher—turned to watch. One of the waitresses disappeared into the kitchen where my grandmother was busy with dinner preparations. I turned my back to her and stared down at the counter. "Less go, Brandon."

My grandmother appeared. "Karen," she said under her breath, her eyes a wash of stone. "Why don't you go on next door? No sense you being in here now. Go on, now." All the customers pretended not to watch.

My face shot red and I stared at my drink.

My mother fumbled with a cigarette and lighter, swaying back and forth, ignoring her.

"Karen—"

"What?" she shot sharply.

"Go on, now, before it gets any worse."

"Oh, *I* need to leave? Is that it, Mother? I don't think so!" She flicked her thumb over the lighter but failed to generate a flame.

"Lower your voice."

"Don't tell me to lower my voice, Mother. I'm talking with my son here, if you don't mind."

"Go, Mom," I said.

"You watch your mouth."

"Look at you," my grandmother said. "You're a damn mess."

"Ain't you one to talk, Mother-dear." Giving up on the smoke, she dropped the lighter into her leather purse.

"You want me to call the police? Is that what you want? Because I will," my grandmother said in a flat, steady voice. "Now, you go and do whatever it is you need to do, but he is staying here."

Right then, my mother snatched my wrist and pulled me from the barstool. I grabbed the counter with my free hand and tried to hold on. My grandmother clutched my shirt. Two or three customers stood as if they might step in. I tried to shake loose but my mother's nails dug into my wrist, puncturing my skin until small crescent blood-moons emerged. Then in one clamorous motion she and I spilled through the café and out the doorway on to the sidewalk, straight into the clearest kind of daylight. She secured her

20

grip on my wrist and started dragging me toward the Enders bar, one door down. I fought and cried, and for the first time in my life, I hit back. The bar door was open and I stayed myself in the doorway, hooking my sneakered feet at the edges of the jamb, my one hand gripping its frame. Inside, shadows and silhouettes moved in the darkness, and I feared that if she pulled me in, I wouldn't come out. That is when my grandmother jerked her away. "Enough is goddamned enough!" Her words fired like pistons.

"Get your hands off of me," my mother barked.

"You horse's ass."

I started to bawl.

Two or three people eyed the drama and moved on. Finally, my mother relented and vanished into the bar, and my grandmother took me into the apartment and tried to talk me through it, tried to tell me everything was okay. I couldn't hear a word over my sobbing and the pain of my wrist. When I calmed down, she left me and went back to work while my mother wiled the rest of the day and night away in the bar. I curled into the shape of an S on my bed, my wrist pinned beneath me, and fell into a deep sleep.

The next day, over what must have been a raging hangover, my mother stepped into my grandparents' apartment where I was flipping through a *Condor-Man* comic book. She sat down and lit a cigarette. Her hands, I noticed, were shaking, but I said nothing. I just stared at my comic book.

"I want to apologize, Brandon. For *that*."

I nodded and felt my face fill with blood.

"I cannot tell you how sorry I am. I don't remember everything I said or did, but I know it was bad, and I know you deserve better."

Again, I said nothing, not knowing what to say.

My mother took a long trembling drag from her cigarette, set it in an ashtray, and took her glasses off to wipe her eyes. She replaced them and lowered her voice even though we were the only ones in the apartment. "Brandon," she said. "All my life I told myself—after watching Grandma and Grandpa beat the holy living hell out of each other, after all the drunken fights, and all the shit—I told myself I would never, never, never be like that when I was a mother. And yet here I am." Her voice cracked and she looked away. I held my gaze steady on the comic book.

"So, I want you to know something. I have talked with your dad, and I have talked with Grandpa, and Buddy and I have decided to quit drinking. We. Are. Done. Because, I will tell you something, Brandon, I will not have you grow up the way I did." She looked off into a blank space. "It's got to stop. It's got to stop. I will not put you through that. I won't. I refuse." She picked up her cigarette and took another drag and exhaled, her resolve unwavering.

I don't remember giving much credence to her pledge, but I don't remember thinking it was an empty promise, either. But after she stubbed out her cigarette and left, I stared at my comic book whose images blurred out of focus.

6. Initiation

The remaining weeks of that summer teemed with energy. There was so much to be done and so much to explore and so many names to learn. Effectively, there were three separate businesses running inside the building and each, to some extent, was its own mysterious world that had its own set of rules and codes. The hotel attended to the roughnecks and drifters who could only afford the seventeen dollar charge on rooms. The café attended to a cast of inveterate locals whose individual stories were intermingled with everyone else's, each one a thread of an enormous web. I learned not to stare at Bruce Murray's mangled thumb, the one that looked like a small red pear, the one he caught in a tractor's whirring power-take-off, or PTO. I learned the story about Kenny Call, the mumbling man who was asked to leave every time he tried to come in. He wore a baseball hat with the visor pulled down over his eyes and kept a network of strings tied to his belt loops. Sometimes he would tie a coffee mug to his belt and it would wag with his uneven gait. "A horse kicked him in the head when he was a kid," I was told when I asked what was wrong with him. "Scrambled him. He's a grown man with the mind of an eight-year-old," my grandmother said. The second or third time he came into the Enders with a mirror on his sneaker, a device he used to stare up the skirts of our waitresses, he was eighty-sixed. Even then he didn't listen. Once when I was on the third story fetching something for my grandfather, I heard a man talking at the end of the hallway. There was Kenny standing there alone, hands jammed into the pockets of his dirty sagging jeans, talking incomprehensibly with his back to me. He shifted his weight from one foot to the other and it appeared as if he was talking to the floor. I took one slow deep breath, stepped backwards, and bolted down the hallway to the staircase, which I flew down. "He does that," my grandfather said miserably. "He wanders those hallways till hell won't have it." One day my grandmother came into the café and saw him bent over by the jukebox fingering the change return for coins. Dismayed, she walked behind him and kicked him square in the butt. "Get out and stay out. I mean it, Kenny."

I learned other things, too, like how not to stare at Don's eye which was permanently swollen and closed shut like he had a golf ball lodged in the socket. And not to stare at Gene Sandwick, the man who sounded like a robot when he talked. "Tracheotomy," I was told. Later, I was introduced to Charlie and Rita, a nice elderly couple who came in for lunch and ordered the same thing every day. "You folks enjoy your lunch," my grandmother said and guided me into the kitchen. And then, when we were out of earshot, she said, "They can't read. That's why they order the same thing, always."

Each business demanded the constant work of reconstruction.

And here I got to help. Mostly my role was gofer. *Run to room 50* (four flights of stairs) *and grab an extension cord. Run downstairs* (five flights of stairs from the third story) *and bring up the stepladder. The chalk line. The level. The square. The pipe wrench. The jigsaw.* I may have groaned at the thought of humping it double-time down five flights of stairs, and five back up, but I was happy. It was an exciting time. There was always something going on in those days.

Everything was in motion. I enjoyed most of all walking into the café for a soda break, taking pride in my dirty clothes and dirty hands—traits that betokened hard work—and hoping customers could see in me the kind of work ethic for which my grandparents were known. Invariably, one of the coffee drinkers—Lloyd, say, who worked for the city and whose hat was perpetually cocked to one side, or Dale, a quiet man, and janitor at the court house—would see me and say, "You working hard or hardly working?"

"I think I'm the only one working around here!"

"Atta boy," he'd say, and return to the *Caribou County Sun* which he held wide open like a kite over his coffee.

Although some of the renovations were readily noticeable, each new repair was inevitably followed by another problem, another leaking pipe, hole in the roof, blinking light. Our lives were patterned on reconstruction.

As a seven-year-old boy and only child, I had the run of the place and ultimately relied on my imagination and a monstrous building to entertain me when I wasn't a gofer. I acted out any number of boyhood fantasies in the Enders.

I found an attaché case in the basement that I filled with crayoned drawings, maps of downtown Soda Springs that I sketched from the vantage point of an upstairs window. In the case I stowed a cap gun, a coil of rope, and a pair of plastic binoculars I bought at Eastman Drug down the street. From dozens of hotel room windows on the third-story (which was still, and always would be, under construction), I spied on the people in the streets and pretended that they were bad guys. I peered through my blurry plastic binoculars, jotted random notes (god knows what), centered the bead of my .38 Special cap gun on many unwitting passersby, uttering *pow, pow, pow, pow* on each shot, afraid of actually pulling the trigger for the sound of the popping caps.

Often I would open a window delighting in how the breeze blew in, tugging at the white curtains. Alone, I would simply stare outward as if seeing the world for the first time. The Idanha Theater across the street, the towering grain elevators to the north, and beyond them, cloaked in smoke, Monsanto. From that window I could see rooftops and weeping willows swaying in the afternoon wind and the buildings scattered around City Park: the firehouse, Presbyterian Church, the bank, and so on. And beyond it all were hills lengthening out into the white horizon, and Mt. Sherman, and the darkening canyons and barley fields. I must have spent an hour in that window, elbows propped on its sill, chin in my hands, breathing in the whiffs of asphalt and the scent of grilled foods that rose from a giant exhaust hood on the roof.

I liked to enter and exit the building in different ways, using various access points so that no two entrances or exits would be the same. I took full advantage: the fire escape (which was little more than a clattery system of ladders and grated platforms that hung off the back of the building); the cement supply-chute, smooth as skin, that emptied into the café basement; the dumb waiter that hoisted cased goods (and me) from the café basement one story up into the back of the kitchen. In all there were sixteen different entrances into the building, sixteen different ways to come and go. And each one I knew intimately.

If I spent a span of afternoons prowling through the dim hotel, I spent double that time outside, on Geyser Hill. Directly behind the Enders Hotel rises a hill, as long as a football field and half as wide, some thirty feet above the city streets. Formed in solid orange rock, Geyser Hill is denuded of vegetation. From its center, a geyser—comparable in size to Old Faithful—erupts at the stroke of every hour. In the 1930s, city engineers started construction on a natatorium, an elaborate edifice housing a large natural swimming pool. They had scarcely drilled fifty feet when the ground started rumbling and steam shot up from its fumarole in a roar. Within minutes they had unleashed a geyser right in the middle of town. As the town flooded with warm, ankle-deep water that smelled like sulfur, befuddled engineers drafted plan after plan to tame this geological force. Eventually they capped it, set it on a timer, and ever since that day it has shot skyward every hour on the hour. That geyser, the official emblem of Soda Springs, was to become my backyard.

As the name suggests, Soda Springs is defined by its waters, by the cold bubbling springs that roil out of its rocky landscape. It is a strange country washed in bright oranges, reds, browns, and greens, the hues of which seem otherworldly. If you go there today you can drive north to the edge of town, toward Monsanto, to Hooper Springs where you can dip a watering can deep into a cold bubbling spring, and drink the fizzing waters. Or stay in town and walk to Octagon Spring (named for the eight-sided gazebo built around it) and do the same. Walk one block north of Octagon Spring to Lover's Delight and take another drink down by the shady banks of Soda Creek, a slow, lazy stream lush with watercress.

As a boy I would come to know only seven or eight prominent springs in and around the town. In the late nineteenth century, however, it was reported that over one hundred springs (some warm but mostly cold) had been identified in the Soda Springs vicinity—none of them suitable for irrigation. Tagged with names like Champaign Spring, Horseshoe Spring, Barrel Spring, Mammoth Spring, Formation Spring, Steamboat Spring, Sulphur Spring, Iron Spring, Ninety-Percent Spring, and Mineral Heights Spring, these waters once promised a place of resort on par with European spas. The settlement's original name was Beer Springs until a group called the Morrisites—a splinter sect of the Mormon Church—moved into the valley and opted for a less scandalous name for the valley's central village. Without question, though, it was the reputation of its waters that kept Soda Springs on the map.

I would wait at the top of the hour near the bubbling blow-hole for the geyser to erupt. I could always hear it before I saw it, and I would scamper back, thrilled by the spectacle. Once it reached its peak height (then between 80 to 150 feet high), I would chuck

27

rocks into the white water and watch them shoot skyward. I got so daring, in fact, that I would touch my trembling fingers to the roaring white column. Its force was so great that my fingertips skipped across its surface, and when I retracted them, they were reddened, stung, and sore. I loved that I could feel the earth's vibrations through the soles of my wet sneakers, and the low grumble of the geyser in my chest, that stinking sulfurous water on my face.

At the base of Geyser Hill stood a squat, single-room basalt rock hut topped with a shingled hexagonal roof. It featured a rear window and a narrow wooden door fixed with a latch and clasp. Inside was a dirt floor and a ceiling covered with flattened cardboard boxes punctuated with hornet nests. Originally built as an above-ground root-cellar for the café, this small building (which I had immediately claimed, and my grandfather granted, as my clubhouse) remained cool during the hot summer. And while reconstruction went on in the Enders Hotel, so did I begin work on the clubhouse. Every day during those last weeks of sun-bled summer, I worked.

With the money I earned for gofering, I bought a padlock and some red spray paint. I took the goods directly to the clubhouse where the first thing I painted on the stone wall, the first thing that surfaced, was a giant red swastika. Like many seven-year-olds, I had little to no understanding of the Third Reich, of Hitler, and had absolutely no conception of the Holocaust. But I loved the ideas of war and soldiers, the uniforms and helmets, the gleam of bayonets. Whenever images of the Nazi ss. appeared on television, marching in step, I couldn't look away. And for all the times my family poked their heads into the building, not a word was said about that red symbol. Not even from my grandfather, who was stationed in Germany during the war.

I recovered a five gallon bucket in the hotel basement that I used for a stool, and I hid my attaché case in the fort as well. Sometimes I would buy an *Archie* comic at Eastman Drugstore and read it in the fort while drinking a can of grape soda, safe in my cavernous quiet.

7. Guns

When I wasn't exploring the hallways and corridors of the hotel, or the geyser and its geothermic mysteries, I prowled around town, thumbed through books at the public library down the street, or bought candy at the drugstore. Early on, my grandparents sent me on numerous errands around town—to Food Town for some item the café had run out of; to Western Auto for a tool or part; to Eastman Drug to pick up various prescriptions (Soda Springs was still small-town enough to allow such things). We had charge accounts all over town so I never carried cash. But I always, always, always had to return with a receipt. And not just the cash register slip. It had to be a fully itemized, hand-written receipt. Later, when Dad took over the books, this became one of his obsessions: the written receipt. Dated, categorized, and annotated. There wasn't an expense in all that building that couldn't be tracked through a labyrinthine paper trail. Every meal ticket issued in the café—large family dinners down to a single cup of coffee—was saved and bundled together with others and stored by month and year in large trash bags in the café basement. Dozens of trash bags held all these tickets. The theory was that if the

IRS came poking around, my grandfather would lead them to the basement, point to the bags, and proudly say, *Have at it. It's all right there.* "If those crooked sons-a-bitches want a hunt, I'll give them one they won't forget," my grandfather would say referring to the IRS. On this point—that the IRS and the government generally were crooked, rotten, liars—my dad and grandfather eagerly agreed. Their hatred of the government drew them closer together. In Washington, for instance, my mother and dad had gone to some seminar on the illegality and unconstitutionality of taxes. This hatred for bureaucrats was one of the many fires that burned deep inside my dad. For my grandfather, it wasn't so much hatred that guided his actions, but a desire to legally "outsmart the bastards at their own game."

So behind each request to run an errand was this feverish single-minded insistence on the written receipt. I didn't mind. In fact, it made me feel important and soon—within a couple of weeks even—I got to know some of the key business people in town.

One place I liked to visit was Western Auto. Something of a general implement, it was located about a block down the street from the Enders. It was large and open with high ceilings and hardwood floors and carried bicycles, pocket knives, tools, guns, pots and pans, sleeping bags, and fishing rods. Mr. Marchant, a short, gray-haired man who wore white, short-sleeved button-down shirts and slacks and who ate regularly at the Enders Café, owned the store and knew me by name. One day, I spotted a black pellet pistol in his display case tagged at nineteen dollars. The price seemed impossibly out of my range, but I wanted that gun so much that it had become something of an obsession. Daily, I made my rounds: clubhouse, Geyser Hill, Geyser Park, Eastman Drug (strawberry milkshake and a bag of Whoppers), and finally Western Auto where I ogled the pistol through the glass.

"Is today the day?" Mr. Marchant would ask, chuckling.

"I wish."

I began saving the money I earned from gofering—stashing it in a cigar box that I stowed beneath my rollaway bed in the corner of the living room—and, in a couple of weeks, I made the purchase. The pistol shot not only pellets, but BBs, and small feathered darts as well. When I left the store I paid no attention to the sounds of the day: the bells that clinked against Mr. Marchant's glass door, the sprinklers in the city park across the street, the bark of a distant dog, the hum of lawnmowers. I could hear only my own heartbeat as I raced back to my clubhouse.

Even as a seven-year-old, I knew my mother hated handguns, but I did not know why exactly.

"It shoots pellets, BBs, and darts!" I told her the day I got it. We were in my grandparents' apartment where she sat on the couch. She lit a cigarette, crossed her legs, and wagged her foot intently—an unfailing mannerism of irritation and a sure sign of her acerbity. After taking a full drag from her cigarette, she said, "I don't care what it does. I don't really care for it, and I tell you what—if anything happens, it's gone. That much is certain."

My mother had her reasons to distrust and fear the presence of guns—air-powered or not—in all their glint and stock. A series of events beyond what had happened in the Enders Bar had led to her fear, like the time when she was a girl on the ranch and Bruce, a lanky farmhand who quartered in the bunkhouse, buried the barrel of a pistol in his mouth and pulled the trigger. The shot sent up a storm of birds from the crab apple trees and could be heard from the ranch house dinner table. My mother remembers cleaning up the mess, the sodden rags she burned in the trash barrels, and the clot of blood-smoke that churned against the sky. Or the time her uncle reached for his holster on the top shelf of his closet, and when it slipped, his thumb caught the trigger and discharged a round into his throat. Or her cousin who shot himself—perhaps accidentally—in the stomach and nearly died. Or when they were living in the green clapboard on the ranch and one of my uncles was playing with a deer rifle in the living room. My mother, LaNae and Marcia (her two sisters), and my grandmother were in the kitchen preparing

31

dinner. My mother had gone to a cupboard to grab a plate when my uncle squeezed the trigger on the rifle. The bullet entered a painting on the living room wall—an oil picture showing mustangs thundering across a floodplain—shot through the kitchen cupboard where only seconds earlier my mother had been standing, and lodged in the far kitchen wall. No one was hurt although a fragment from one of the dinner platters nicked my mother's cheek. A large plastic oval featuring a picture of a big-breasted turkey, the platter sustained a hole right through its center, effectively killing the turkey. And so the joke always went that my uncle missed one of the thundering mustangs but got himself a turkey. That painting, complete with its bullet hole the size of a pencil eraser, hung in the café dining room not far from where Charlie was shot some years earlier, and the platter was stored in a box in the hotel basement.

Shortly after I bought the pellet pistol, I was in the clubhouse reading comic books when I heard voices just outside the door. Standing up quietly, I peered through a small peephole and saw two kids I did not recognize, maybe twelve or thirteen years old. I began to panic when they approached and began prying at the door. The small bolt-lock on the inside rattled. They could not have known what awaited them, that inside I clutched the new pellet pistol and aimed its shaking barrel at the door. I had been haunted by a story my grandmother told me weeks earlier, one of urban legend proportions, but one whose horrifying details I took to be true. It was a story about two men who cornered a boy (about my age) in a rest area, beat him up, and cut off his "thing." That was my grandmother's word for the penis: *his thing*. I did not sleep for days, so terrified was I by that story. The moral was simple: stay the hell away from strangers if you want to keep your thing.

When they broke the inner-lock loose, the door swung open and the two kids stumbled backwards wide-eyed at the sight of a kid brandishing a shaking pistol that looked identical to a .45 magnum (my grandfather had drawn the comparison). "Jesus! He's got a gun! Don't shoot!"

32

I felt my face flush and the blood burn through my eardrums. My conviction was steady even if my grip on the pistol wasn't. "Get out of here," I said. "And don't you ever come back!"

The two kids turned and bolted through the gravel parking lot toward the drugstore and that was the last time I ever saw them. About thirty minutes later, however, a police car rolled into the lot and an officer stepped out, and shut his door behind him. I was standing in the golden weeds that fringed the stony clubhouse, trying, but failing, to appear innocent. His hair was dark and curly and he wore thick glasses and a mustache.

"This your clubhouse?" He asked.

The police radio squawked in the background.

I nodded and then swallowed hard. "Yeah."

He looked around casually as if taking in the scenery. "Got a complaint that you're over here waving a gun around. This true?"

"Not really. But sort of."

He settled his gaze on me and said, "Well, it's either true or it's not. So which is it?"

I said nothing but felt myself nodding as my knees turned rubbery. Fearing to make eye contact, I stared at my tennis shoe and toed a clump of June grass. The sun was hot on my back and on my neck, and I felt sick inside.

"Why don't you tell me where this gun is, son."

I pointed to the clubhouse. The police officer stuck his head into the dark, narrow doorway, squirmed in and emerged with my black pistol.

"It's just a pellet gun," I muttered.

I told him what had happened and he gave me a very earnest lecture on the dangers of guns—pellet guns included: "people have been killed by pellet guns before"—and let me go with a warning.

I never told anyone about that afternoon, and as the days tumbled on, it became clear that nothing would come of the incident, and I was relieved.

8. Apparition

One day that summer a kid named Ernie appeared out of no-where. The wind was blowing and the day was thick with heat and wind and the tall grass around the geyser rustled in the gentle gusts. He was maybe two years older than me and his hair was longish like mine. I was outside my clubhouse at the base of Geyser Creek and I was alone. It was as if I was the only person for miles around, and then all of a sudden there was this smirking kid named Ernie standing in front of me. An apparition. He walked right up to me and said, "You're Brandon, right?"

I was stunned. "Yeah. How'd you know my name?"

"Your Grandpa Lynn calls you The Brat."

I laughed nervously.

"I'm Ernie," he said as if that should have cleared up every-thing.

I stared at him blank-faced.

"Patrick's son? Patrick John?"

"Oh, yeah—I've heard of you, I think."

I knew Patrick John. He was my mother's best friend, or one of them, from long ago, back when she and my father, Jerry, were still together. They had all lived together for a short time with two other friends in a trailer near Idaho Falls, Idaho. Six in all, most of them in their late teens, drop-outs and hot-heads, they passed their time in a haze of drunken and drug-smudged nights. Then my mother started throwing up in the mornings. That is when she left Jerry the first time. Moved back to Soda Springs. But she and Patrick stayed in touch.

Ernie looked like Patrick. And he was nice in a way that was strangely menacing. Here was this kid I had never seen before who seemed to know more about me than I did. We spent the afternoon together and he related stories to me about my mother and me and my grandparents and his father and I just laughed the whole time because I didn't know what to say. By the end of the day I was looking at him closely. His face and fair complexion, his hair, his eyes, and his nose, and slowly, I started to build the case in my mind that this kid who sat next to me in the Enders Café—this Ernie kid who fell from the sky—was in fact my brother, and that Patrick John was my father. That it had been Patrick all along. I had convinced myself that we even looked the same, Ernie and I, and that Patrick and I looked alike. It all made sense to me. I had a father and, better yet, an older brother. That night I formulated a list of questions I would ask Ernie the next day, questions that might reveal more of the story and confirm what I had suspected. That night I went to sleep with high hopes, but I never saw Ernie again.

9. Generations

The walkout was still in effect. While Dad was happy to have work and twelve-hour shifts, the commute to Pocatello was draining him, and the union wage scale wasn't as high as it was at Hanford. He wanted to get back. Besides, he was paying rent on an uninhabited house in the southeastern desert of Washington State. "Any word of when we might start up?" he would say into the phone, his pen and notebook at the ready. The answer was invariably the same: *Hard to say, Bud. Could be three days. Could be three weeks. Could be three months.*

Often in the evenings I would see Dad and my grandfather talking in my grandparents' apartment. Rather my grandfather did most of the talking while Dad nodded attentively. My mother and grandmother had similar conversations over coffee and cigarettes. I didn't recognize these conversations for what they were. My parents were trying to heal themselves after years of reckless drinking and they had turned to two people who themselves had put an end to their own alcoholic abandon. My grandfather had started an AA chapter in Soda Springs shortly before he and my grandmother bought the Enders. A plaque on his office wall hanging above his safe read: *God grant me the serenity to accept the things I cannot change; the courage to change the things I can, and the wisdom to know the difference.*

I thought it was a poem so I would always pause in his office to read its words. It wasn't long before I had it memorized.

Those evening conversations held more than just the vestiges of recovery, though. I couldn't name it or identify it as such, but there was an earnestness and quietude about those long talks that said something about reconnecting. As an only child, I hovered at the periphery of this adult world with my attention split between a toy or comic and their words which were drawn out over thick clouds of cigarette smoke. There was something hauntingly tentative about it all.

Summer receded and harvest chaff hung in the air in great golden clouds. Flecks of earth flung into the wind and the days burned slow. And so the walkout at Hanford continued into the school year. I was nervous and filled with equal amounts of dread and anticipation about attending a new school. With the exception of Ernie and visits to my cousin's yellow clapboard house on the ranch, I passed that summer mostly alone or among the world of adults, and so I looked forward to a world of boys.

My second grade class in Soda Springs was astonishing and memorable only because nearly one third of the class was named Brandon. It seems uncanny and even impossible to me now that we had seven Brandons in one room in such a small town. My mother was proud that I was the oldest out of all of them, that she had thought of the name first. It must have been maddening for Mrs. Jones to contend with us all. She was a tall, fey woman whose dark, stringy hair brushed over her shoulders, and who spoke through a red nose that looked sore. She must have thought it was a cruel joke when she received her roster and scanned the litany of Brandons.

Brandon Bailey
Brandon Burnham

Brandon Fulton

Brandon Harding

Brandon Porter

Brandon Schrand

Brandon Weaver

One day Mrs. Jones stood at the blackboard during a lesson in penmanship. I had been talking or otherwise not listening when her shrill reprimand singled me out. Sitting in the front row, red-faced and injured, I shoved my desk so hard that it tipped over and slammed to the floor. Its heavy lid broke off completely and everything inside spilled out onto the floor: my cigar box of crayons, pencils, and Matchbox cars; phonics papers, my glue bottle, scissors, sharpener, and workbooks. Everything. Then Mrs. Jones was the one who looked injured and most of all, horrified. She snatched me under my arm and jerked me down the hall to the office. I bawled as my legs gave way. The principal had called the café and got hold of my grandfather. "You need to come get him," he had said. "We simply cannot have this."

I spent no more than a single day sitting out of school for my performance, and was met with the usual questions one would expect for such an episode. "What has gotten into you? Why would you go and do such a thing? You know better than to behave like that!"

I hung my head. The only thing I could say was *sorry*.

When I returned to Mrs. Jones's class, I had a new desk with all of my stuff dumped inside. All the kids looked at me when I entered the room, but Mrs. Jones went about the day's lesson as if nothing had happened, her voice overly bright and guarded.

At recess, one of the Brandons approached me on the playground. "You get in trouble?" he asked.

"Sorta."

"Yeah, well, she's a bitch anyway."

Caught off guard, I laughed, and snorted. I liked him immediately because he talked to me and took my side. But mostly because he swore. That was exciting.

"I'm B.J.," he said. His moppish dark hair hung in his blue eyes, and he was slightly bigger than me, a fact that seemed accentuated by his Los Angeles Rams jersey.

"Your last name is Weaver, right?"

"Yeah. But my middle name is John. Brandon John—B.J. That's what everyone calls me."

"I guess that would make me B.R. My middle name is Russell." The origin of my middle name has always struck me as odd. When my mother delivered me she was so "out of it," as she says, that she named me after the doctor: Russell Tigert, the primary physician in Soda Springs at the time. Years later, whenever Dr. Tigert dined in the café, I ducked out, embarrassed somehow. On the playground that day, however, I spared B.J. the story.

B.J. considered B.R. as a nickname and said, "Nah. You're B.S. It sounds better." (In class I was simply *Brandon S.*)

B.S. *did* sound better than B.R., certainly. "Cool," I said. "B.S. I like that." I had never had a nickname before (although Grandpa called me The Brat, it didn't count. It was nothing I could take to school).

That afternoon we walked home together, taking a detour through a draw and along a creek bank choked with willows and cattails. We chucked rocks into the water, threw sticks, and talked endlessly. He asked where I lived and I said the Enders Hotel. "We own it," I said looking toward S-Hill, that rose to the north.

"Wow. You must be rich."

"Not really," I said. "Not really at all."

When the autumn afternoon sun warmed us in a wash of yellow light, we walked up from the creek bank to the road and said our goodbyes.

That evening, my family and I sat around a table in the café's dining room, and had dinner. "I met a friend today," I said. "One of the Brandons. Except he goes by B.J.—Brandon John. That's his middle name, John. His last name is Weaver. Said his dad is an electrician—like Dad."

"I'll be damned," my grandmother said. "That's Rex and Jane's grandson."

My grandfather nodded and wiped his mouth with a napkin. "Beaver Weaver's boy," he said smiling. "Didn't you work with Beaver out to Becker a few years ago, Bud?"

"Yeah. Yeah, I know old Beaver," Dad said.

"Beaver Weaver? Is that his *real* name?" I laughed and picked up my cheeseburger.

"No, his name is Allen," my mother said.

"He used to run around with us kids a lot," my mother said.

"So why do they call him Beaver?"

"Because he could open beer bottles with his teeth."

I got parts of the story over dinner, the rest over the years. How our grandparents used to prowl the back roads into the darkening throat of Wood Canyon on our ranch as they spotlighted for elk. How inside the truck cab the two couples passed beers back and forth under a crescent moon, told stories, and flicked cigarette ashes into the tray that opened from the dash like a steel jaw. How they played poker on Friday nights at the green clapboard ranch house, and danced at Stockman's Tavern on Saturdays as they sucked down smokes and knocked back finger after finger of Black Velvet. And how Beaver and my mother and my uncles and aunts dragged Main Street on the weekends, boosted liquor from their parents' cabinets and drank it over bonfires up at Swan Lake. While many of the details of our families' meshed histories were revealed over time, I got a sense that night that my new friendship with B.J. was generational. It was inherited, the rarest of things.

The next day at school B.J. said, "Our grandparents are like best friends!"

"I know! And your dad and my dad worked together, and my mom and uncles and aunts used to hang out with your dad!"

We never said aloud that all of this made us best friends. We didn't need to. It had been handed to us. Just like that. Here was someone with whom I could share my stories.

B.J. lived in a white clapboard postwar home across the street from the Thriftway supermarket. A large box elder tree shaded the front yard and a small, sagging garage hunkered on the south side of the house. Their backyard was an open, if unkempt wash of grass, and the back fence—wooden, weathered, and failing—abutted a trailer park.

Their house bustled with people on their way in or out. B.J.'s older brother, David, a gregarious, confident kid with wavy blonde hair who always traveled in the company of two or three gangly, freckle-faced friends; and his younger brother, Darren, a defensive five-year-old whose constant whining earned him beatings from B.J., David, and later, me. Pictures of the three boys hung on their living room wall next to the picture of a fourth boy who wore David's blond hair but looked like B.J. The fourth boy flashed a quixotic smile despite a missing front tooth. "Who's that?" I asked the first afternoon I spent over there.

"That's my brother Robert," B.J. said. "He was killed on a snowmobile. Hit a fencepost and broke his neck."

"Oh," I said, stunned, sick that I had asked.

"He was only twelve."

"Sorry," I said.

Although they talked of him as if he had been dead for years, it occurs to me now, if I do the math, that his death had to have been recent, his absence still an open wound in that house. Years later I would speculate that Robert's death marked the first of many fractures for the Weaver family. B.J. told me as much once, intimating how they could never know again that kind of innocence they knew when Robert was alive. In the Weaver family mythology it was Robert who had died for their sins.

"He was great," B.J. said as we stared at the picture. "He was the greatest kid you could have met. Did anything Mom and Dad told him to."

David overheard us from the kitchen and walked in holding an egg salad sandwich. "Yeah. He wasn't like us. We bitch and moan whenever we're asked to help out."

"Watch your mouth," their mother called softly from the kitchen.

I liked their mother. She was kind and funny and vaguely attractive with long dark hair, olive skin, and winsome eyes.

I remember when I first met their dad, Beaver, and how I thought he was frightening somehow, and hilarious—wild, like he still had too much kid in his adult-sized body. He was loud and gruff, awash in tattoos from Vietnam. His hair was dark brown and I never saw him without a cigarette dangling loosely from his mouth.

"Dad, this is B.S.," B.J. said when I met him.

Covered in axle grease, Beaver stood in their front yard working on their car, a Maroon 1970s Toronado. Its huge hood yawned open, and a beer was parked on the bumper. He wore a red, sleeveless T-shirt and cut-off jeans.

"B.S., huh? Sounds like Bullshit to me!" He laughed and B.J. and I laughed, and I could feel my face turn red.

"Well, it's good to meet you, B.S."

"You, too."

"What are you two up to today besides trouble?"

"B.S. has a clubhouse down at the Enders we're going to fix up."

"Lynn and Beth know about it?"

"Oh, yeah," I said. "They said we could."

Beaver nodded and took a slug of beer. "How's your old man doing?"

"Fine, I guess."

"Is he working over to Pocatello?"

"Yep."

"That's good." He drained the beer and flung the can into the grass. "Got to take what you can get." He turned back to the engine. "Well," he said, "tell everyone I said hello."

"Okay."

42

"See ya, Dad," B.J. said and we trailed off for the Enders Hotel.

Everything seemed right, and I was beginning to sense my place in the order of things and this gave me such a deep feeling of comfort that as we walked, the wind on my face felt like gratitude itself.

Because of its dirt floor, the fort always smelled like earth, rich and dank. Its rock walls felt cool and we could climb them up to the ceiling. Late that afternoon we goofed around out by the clubhouse, throwing rocks and green beer bottles into the geyser when it erupted. The bottles shot eighty feet or higher into the air, sending us scampering with our hands clamped over our heads. To us the shattered glass didn't look like trash. It looked like jewels, something rare.

Soon we found ourselves hiking over Geyser Hill and into the Fairview Cemetery. The graveyard would fast become part of our domain. Weeping willows, cottonwoods, juniper, and lilac trees shaded much of the cemetery, and small, graveled roads formed a grid that we would come to know by heart. To the north side, the geyser runoff gurgled by in a mineral orange creek bed that ran parallel to the nearby railroad tracks. Beyond the tracks, fields of sagebrush and more juniper swept out for miles, broken only by Soda Creek or the occasional barbed wire fence that slouched in the brush.

In the cemetery, as if the setting called for it, we broke into an impromptu game of war. Each of us brandished a broken tree branch as a fully automatic M-16. We ran and jumped headstones, shinnied up trees only to drop out and topple to the ground. We darted between junipers yelling *Go, go, go, go!* And *Move out!* We waved our arms dramatically at invisible troop detachments as we fought our way to a rendezvous point. I remember lying belly-down in the freshly mown grass behind a headstone and aiming my stick, muzzle-first, at an enemy foxhole. B.J., I noticed, kept moving his troops to the southwest corner of the cemetery, into the new section, where no trees grew. I liked the older section of

43

the graveyard where it was shaded and close to the geyser, but decided to follow anyway. I moved in perfect stealth mode, diving here and there, darting between fragrant junipers. And that's when I saw B.J. kneeling before a small stone, talking. I dropped my stick and approached. I hadn't thought about it until that very moment, but his brother, Robert, lay buried there in the newest part of the cemetery, the part with no trees.

"I miss him," he said.

Not knowing what to say, not having the words, I just nodded.

"Well, see ya," B.J. said to the stone. "We're gonna go now."

He stood and we walked along a length of gravel road to the old part of the cemetery where the weeping willows swayed, and at the creek we tossed in the crooked branches and watched them float away and then disappear.

10. The Boxer

Some time after we saw Robert's headstone in the cemetery, B.J. came over and we headed into the café for a soda. The café was bright with yellow-white light crashing through the two large picture windows at the front. One of our waitresses, Tootie, stood at the lunch counter rolling silverware into napkins. She had long dark hair, impeccably done, and was, I thought, attractive. Two or three customers wiled away the afternoon over cups of coffee, and the afternoon cook, Joyce, a large woman with meaty arms and broomish red hair, sat at the break table smoking a cigarette. She was nice, but could be at times shockingly dim-witted. Once she tried to free a piece of toast from the toaster with a butter knife despite my mother's harried warnings. When she jammed the blade into the glowing slot, she shrieked, and flung the knife across the kitchen.

B.J. and I took two barstools where Tootie was working.

"Hello, boys," she said. "What can I get you?"

"I'll just have some water," B.J. said.

"You can have whatever you want," I said in a sidelong whisper.

"I don't got any money, though."

45

"Don't worry about it. I'm having a Coke. What are you having?"

"I'll have a Coke, too," he said, pleased no doubt by this kind of access.

"Two Cokes," Tootie said. "Are we eating, too, or just the Cokes?"

"Pie sounds good," I said.

B.J. looked at me and chuckled nervously. "Sure."

Tootie brought out some pie and B.J. was beaming. We spun around on the stools, drinking our cold drinks, eating pie, and discussed plans for the clubhouse. And then plans for a club. I would be president (because the clubhouse was technically mine), and B.J. would be vice president. No girls would be admitted into our order. B.J.'s brother David, might be. Outside of that, we didn't know who else we would or could invite. The smaller, the better, we told ourselves.

Because my grandparents and my mother napped during the afternoon, I was on my own, and so I figured it was a good time to indulge in my favorite pastime: exploring. After we finished our pie and Cokes, and placed our dishes into the gray bus tub at the end of the counter, I said, "Come on. Let's check out the basement."

We slipped off our stools and crossed the café to the doorway that led into the lobby. Always darker than the café, the lobby was generally quiet save the cackle and din that spilled from the bar whose doorway stood on the far side of the lobby, opposite of the café's. On our way through, we noticed a man walking down the red-carpeted stairway. He fished a cigarette from the pack in his shirt pocket and winked at us. He was slim and peppery-haired, donned in war-khakis, wingtips, and a starchy white button-down, his sleeves rolled loosely to his forearm. It was his usual dress. His hands were large and his knuckles looked like stony walnut casings. His face wore the years of a battered paper sack. I tried an awkward smile, said, "Hullo," and we kept walking. Beyond the

46

front desk was the basement door. On it were brass letters that read, "Sample Room"—a reminder of the days when merchants showcased their goods in this center of rural commerce. I swung the large door open, clicked on the light, and we descended the wide wooden staircase. Before we reached the bottom, B.J. said, "Who was that? That guy we saw?"

"Forrest? *He used to be like a famous boxer,*" I whispered.

"Whoa," B.J. said.

"Yeah."

Forrest Jack Barger, or "Kid Barger," was a middleweight champ back in the days when respectable boxing was called prizefighting. He had grown up on a small farm near Preston, Idaho, an agricultural town some forty miles south of Soda Springs. In 1927, at the age of fifteen, Forrest started boxing in the sweaty, smoke-thick Preston Opera House on Saturday nights. For five years he fought in and around southern Idaho and northern Utah, boxing men with names like Tuffy Mecham, Mack Payne, and Mickey McCafferty. After his weekend fights, he would hop a train home where he stacked hay, fed pigs, and irrigated a small crop with sore hands and swollen eyes.

Once at the Stadium in Ogden, Utah, Forrest delivered a TKO punch to Charley Feraci in the first round. The crowd wanted more, so the two boxed another four rounds for the sake of theater. During a fight in Logan, Utah, Frisco McGale knocked Barger down in the first round, but the Kid returned to beat McGale in the ninth.

In the winter of 1932, however, everything would change for Forrest. Jack Dempsey, then former heavyweight champion of the world, took notice of the Kid from Idaho and endorsed him. The newspapers were abuzz with the news of Dempsey's protégé, "the Kid Barger from the wilds of Idaho."

Dempsey sent the Kid east to fight in Philadelphia, the New York Coliseum in the Bronx, and arenas around Boston. Then on

January 13, 1933, he fought the Cuban boxer, Antonio Dominguez in Madison Square Garden. The twenty-one-year-old Forrest Barger beat Dominguez in six rounds. It must have been the biggest night of his life. The crowd would have roared, the cameras flashed. Cigars and drinks all around. And Jack Dempsey would have stood ringside with a towel snapped over his shoulder, proud, perhaps, of this new Kid, his prodigy. Forrest Jack Barger lost only four matches and was never knocked out.

But his career was explosive and ended, it seems, just as quickly as it had begun. Perhaps tired of the newspapers, the white-hot camera flashes, the physical toll of weekly fights, the Kid boarded a train bound for Idaho and put the East and Jack Dempsey behind him. He had three more fights in him, and would win the first two. One in Boise, against Paul Delaney, and another against Hal Hoxwood in Preston where he started. The final match, though, took place in July, 1935 in Ogden, Utah. Before a full crowd, Jackie Burt outpointed Barger and the Kid would end his career on a loss. He spent the rest of his life on a tractor, tending his farm. And over the ensuing years, when he could leave the farm, he would drive to Soda Springs, check into the Enders, and spend two weeks drinking in the bar.

That is how we came to know him.

People knew Forrest had boxed, but he never talked about fighting. He would talk about his farm, but not about the other thing. He had a subtle lisp that was exaggerated with drink, and inevitably, men in the bar would try to goad the seventy-year-old into a fight. "Come on old man," they'd say. "You think you're something? You still got it? Let's see it." But Forrest would stub out his cigarette, finish his whiskey, turn his back on them, and shuffle up the red-carpeted stairway to his room.

"He's a gentleman," Grandma had said whenever I asked about Forrest. "Doesn't cause any problems. But when a person drinks like that, it's best to stay out of their business. Help them if you can, but don't bother them."

To me, though, he simply looked like a member of my grandfather's generation, one of those men who bathed in Old Spice and oiled their hair. But looking back on him now, he seems like someone whom the Rat Pack might have admitted into their silvery confidence but then, over martinis and second thoughts, decided to toss aside.

I never said more than hello to Forrest, never summoned the child's equivalent of courage to do so. But I remember thinking he was something all right—someone who mattered. Someone who had some stories to tell. My God, the stories he must have known.

At the bottom of the stairs, the hallway went left toward the boiler room, coal room, saw-room, and laundry room; or right toward the tool room, storage room, larder, a room I called the suitcase room (on account of the dozens of abandoned suitcases heaped there), the furniture room and into the laundry room completing the loop. We went right, taking the narrow corridor whose cobwebbed ceiling was erratic with pipes and conduit and the occasional caged red glass bulb filled with fluid—an early fire extinguisher. They were scattered throughout the basement.

"This is cool," B.J. said taking in these surroundings. "What's in here?"

"That's the tool room." We stepped inside and clicked on the light. The room was filled with tool boxes, welding gear, grinders, coiled extension cords, and the walls were riddled with hanging wrenches, hammers, screwdrivers, and levels and squares. It was the only room in the basement with a wooden floor.

We stepped back into the hallway and continued into the suitcase room. While some guests bartered for room and board, and others worked off their bills, some—the truly desperate, those trying to outpace the stories they had come to live in—walked away leaving everything behind without a word or gesture as to why. More often than not, they left the most cumbersome of their belongings, the one thing that slowed them down the most: their

49

suitcases. Over the years we had accumulated so many that we set aside this room for their storage, their burial, and in a sense, the room became a kind of mausoleum of the forgotten people who shuffled in and out of our lives—a crypt, a tomb, a potter's field.

Years later, when I started to resent living in the Enders, I would find myself alone in that room, under the jaundiced glow of a single 60-watt bulb. There, I spent hours and days and then weeks unbuckling old suitcases, sifting through musty clothes, reading yellowed letters, and staring into old photographs, locking eyes with strangers who stared back from oblivion. A photograph from the 1950s showed a family a-sprawl on a summer lawn. I imagined they were from some place clean and ordered, some place like Iowa or Indiana. The people in that picture belonged to a family. They lived in a house. They ate dinner around an oak table. Glasses of milk. Pot roast. Heads tilted in prayer. I would eat every meal in a café, by myself, at the counter where I spun around on a barstool, one shoelace untied. But despite their apparent cohesiveness, the American family in the photograph—for all their smiles, striped shirts and farm-boy cowlicks—for all of that, their picture still ended up in an abandoned suitcase in the basement of a rundown hotel in a dust-blown corner of Idaho.

Other pictures arrive to me in a vague dream-state sort of way. An old man leaning against a fence. Perhaps a little girl tips against him. Or a woman who looks like Judy Garland holding a baby up to the camera. How could they have known that a boy mooned over their photographs in a hotel basement for countless hours, and envied them? How could they have known that he would one day grow to be a man and fall away from that hotel? How could they have possibly known any more than I did—or do—that it all falls away eventually, that we all find our course descending the same rungs of that certain human fate: the known, the remembered, and the forgotten?

All I wanted to find was treasure in those suitcases, a thick roll of bills, a pocketknife, jewels. Anything. What I usually found instead was a broken watch, a matchbook, or a brown bottle of cologne in the shape of a roadster or totem pole.

Inside, I threw the light switch. The room itself was huge and filled nearly to the ceiling with stuff—mostly old luggage. But there were other things too. An old menu that used to hang in the café featuring coffee for five cents. A pair of thatched snow shoes, a photo album that contained hundreds of black and white pictures of unknown people. The pictures likely belonged to the Fraser family, who ran the place in the forties and fifties, the people my grandmother waitressed for after she graduated high school. That was another family connection to the Enders.

Boxes of china and teapots were stacked next to the wall. Transistor radios were stacked on adding machines, chairs were perched on other chairs. We rifled through cupboards and cleared shelves. B.J. found a pair of cross country skis, and I found a wooden box with a handle and discovered inside what appeared to be an old shoeshine kit. "Check this out," I said. "We could shine shoes for people in the lobby and probably make a ton of money."

"Easy," B.J. said. "Old guys love to have their shoes shined. And they got money." Guys like Forrest Barger, perhaps. Clearly someone had shined shoes in the Enders at some point. A boy, say, decked in bib overalls, might have hung around the lobby when it was used as the town's bus station, and offered shoeshines to the people arriving from distant places, or those bound for points beyond. It is easy enough to imagine.

B.J. and I looked around at the room piled with boxes and relics. "So like all this stuff's gonna be yours someday? Like the whole place?"

I shrugged at first and said, "I don't know. I guess so." But then I settled into the idea and recast my answer, spinning it some. "I mean, sure. You know. Jade and Angel will get the ranch, and I will get the hotel—that's kind of how it's supposed to work."

"Cool."

On top of a cupboard at the back wall, I spotted a large scroll of paper. I grabbed an old wooden chair, scooted it to the cupboard, climbed up and retrieved it.

"What is it?"

"I don't know."

We crouched to the floor and unrolled it, a map of some sort that measured about three feet by three feet, the size of a window.

"Cool," B.J. said.

It was like no map I had seen before, awash in numbers I took to be coordinates of some sort. It looked like the kind of map a sailor might use. We looked at it closely: Alaska: Dixon Entrance to Cape St. Elias, U.S. Coast & Geodetic Survey, 1929.

"Whoa," we whoaed.

"Look." I pointed to the right side of the map. A list of hand-written notes fell down the side of the map. Each note was numbered and the numeral corresponded to a place on the map.

"Do you think it's a treasure map?" B.J. wondered, his eyes glowing.

"Could be."

We smoothed our hands across its skin and pressed against it as if the act of touching could take us there, could reveal the map's story, its secrets.

"I bet an old sea captain left it here."

A length of silence passed between us as we were lost in our thoughts about this thing.

We rolled up the map and I tucked it carefully under my arm. "Come on. I'll show you the rest of the basement."

I would keep that map for the rest of my life and eventually frame it, believing still in its power to pull me back into a story I have yet to discover.

We stopped at the larder and admired its solid, two-foot-thick wooden door. Inside stood a half dozen water-warped oil paintings, the ones my grandmother wasn't able to salvage. "Those yours?" B.J. asked, gesturing toward the paintings.

I shrugged.

We continued down a corridor, past the furniture room stuffed with old leather rockers, and into the enormous room that contained a dozen old wringer-washing machines and a steam press at the base of a laundry chute. "This is where the laundry comes out," I explained. "Or used to." We peered up the chute but saw nothing more than darkness and the bottom chunk of rope that ran from the third story to the basement. "I've always wanted to climb up the chute," I said. "But I don't dare."

"Yeah. Like what if you got stuck?"

"I know. That would suck." We laughed.

B.J. stuck his head in the chute and took another look. He tested the rope. "I bet we could do it."

"You think?"

"Maybe."

"I don't know. If you got stuck, how would you get out? Besides, I could get in trouble."

I didn't know how we would get out, and in the end, we decided against the idea, a noticeably wise decision for boys whose curiosity would have otherwise trumped fear. That laundry chute has always fascinated me, though. The shaft itself was a good three feet by three feet, yet we could never find a wall on the ground floor thick enough to accommodate that kind of space. For years I puzzled over that shaft and tried to summon the gumption to shimmy up that rope through the darkness.

"I got an idea," I said. "Let's leave the light on down here and go upstairs to the top floor and see if we can see down. Maybe we can see what it will look like."

"Okay."

When we emerged from the basement, I stepped in the apartment and dropped off the nautical map, and then we hit the stairs, running the whole way. A door on the third floor read "Sink," but when you opened it, there wasn't a wash basin, but a different kind of sink: a hole that sunk four stories. It was the laundry chute. We stuck our heads in and peered down. Sure enough we could make out the yellow glow at the bottom, but little else. The rope in the center—around which maids used to tie bundles of dirty linen before they dropped it—was taut, and we tested it with our hands. We were quiet, thinking, no doubt, of the same thing: if we fell, that would be it.

The building would swallow us.

There was always something unsettling about the architecture and general layout of the Enders Hotel, something puzzling. Herman Falkenberg was the lead architect. I wonder about Mr. Falkenberg's vision of this building. I used to wonder if he wasn't a little mad. Now I wonder if he wasn't brilliant. The basement, for instance, contained six dead staircases, three of which led into nothing more than a maze of ceiling beams, pipes, wires, and cobwebs. The other three climbed to trap doors cut in the floor of the ground story. One room in that basement, though, lacked doors or windows or portals of any kind. No access. We found it by chance when tracing a leak in a hot-water pipe. When my grandfather pried boards loose from the wall he discovered behind those planks a small room, as black space fell away from the dusty claws of his hammer. And when he threw his flashlight beam into the room's vacuity his eyes fixed on the only thing in there: another dead staircase.

We found a similar cell behind the larder, a room I dubbed the vault because of its heavy door. But behind that vault's back wall stood another closed off room, and in *that* room stood another dead staircase that ran away to nowhere. As a boy I loved that our basement had secret rooms. I conjured up ideas that whoever planned them did so out of dementia or paranoia. Or for other purposes.

Although I entertained marvelous ideas about those dead staircases, trap doors, and vaulted rooms, it is more likely that they weren't built out of feverish insanity or under the reign of a sweaty mastermind. I suspect something more practical governed their design. The *Chieftain* reports that construction on the Enders started in June 1917, five months after Idaho outlawed booze. It is not a stretch to imagine that the trap doors—easily covered with a rug or a table—could have led to caches of hidden alcohol. Perhaps, too, the trap doors provided quick access to the speakeasy in the basement. There one minute, gone the next. Perhaps William and Theodore Enders held a meeting with Falkenberg. *This is what we want*, they might have said, indicating a world above and the world below. Passageways and passwords. Handshakes and understandings. Perhaps.

Something else about the building. A crawl space large enough to accommodate a slightly stooped adult separated the ground floor from the second floor. It was a floor between floors. And that floor was a labyrinthine network of hallways and corridors, rooms and compartments, nooks and vestibules. Ron Hamp, the plumber we called when the bowels in the building required professional care, got lost in the floor between floors. He was up there for hours, panicked and disoriented. He knocked on walls, hammered on ceiling joists hoping that we would hear him, that we might receive the distress call from beyond. But we didn't. When he finally emerged he was dusty, pale, and shaken. My grandmother laughs about it still. "He was spooked, all right. He didn't think he would ever get out of there."

It was early November and winter was upon us. B.J. and I invented new ways to entertain ourselves. We lobbed snowballs at passing freight trains, raced our sleds (plastic sheets with handles) down the schoolyard slope, and went to movies together where each of us would buy, always, giant dill pickles, spicy pickled sausages, and Cokes. The Idanha Theater stood right across the street from the Enders Hotel.

My family stayed busy during that time, too, and appeared upbeat and happy despite the circumstances afoot, circumstances to which I was not privy. The worsening condition of my grandfather's emphysema, for instance. Although he had quit smoking his Winstons, he refused to go on oxygen. His doctor urged him, emphatically, to use it, supplementally, at least at night. It would help, he said. Afraid of becoming dependent upon a tank, afraid of that kind of entrapment, my grandfather dug in and tried to fight the disease. Inevitably, though, he began to lose ground as everyone knew he would. Drawing a full breath became more and more labored. Eventually, a cold, green, cylindrical tank filled with pure oxygen stood at the head of his bed. I was vaguely frightened of this armless gargoyle towering in my grandparents' room. To me, it looked like a beheaded soldier, a robot, or a bomb that could explode at any given second.

Only those patients who have advanced emphysema are required to go on supplemental oxygen. The disease is particularly menacing because the lungs lose their elasticity. Those afflicted with emphysema are encumbered with the haunting reality that it is not just a progressively arduous task to draw a full breath, but it is increasingly difficult to exhale the breath once they have taken it in. The disease, my grandparents knew, was terminal. This was the part I didn't know. When I had asked about the oxygen tank and the green hoses that hooked into his nose, my grandmother simply said, "Oh, that just helps your grandpa when he needs it."

Other worries no doubt nagged away at them, too. The ranch operations that still provided a large amount of their income. Family matters. Keeping their diseases in check. My grandmother, for instance, had undergone a mastectomy only a few years before, checking herself into the hospital without saying a word to my grandfather. "I didn't want him worrying about it," she said. "It was just one of those things I had to do myself." And faced with my grandfather's diagnosis, they must have felt some anxiety as they carried no health insurance. They had always paid cash. Not to mention the worries over business, of income and expenses, of amassing debt to recover the Enders, and to implement the renovations, but to what end, they must have wondered? To what end?

Life at the Enders Hotel offered enough work that one could easily get lost in the rhythms of the day's demands. If stoicism didn't staunch the flood of worry, work or surprises certainly would. On a random morning, for instance, my grandmother woke, as she did every morning, at four o'clock, showered, dressed, and stepped from the apartment to open the café. Dad had already started his drive to Pocatello in the falling snow. My mother was getting ready for work, and my grandfather was still asleep. And so was I.

The lobby was nearly pitch-black but for the ambient street light that filtered softly through the front windows. It wasn't, however, too dark that morning for my grandmother to miss the body of a man lying face down in the middle of the lobby floor. She stopped short, and caught her breath. Her first thought was that he was dead. Stepping away slowly, she moved backwards toward the apartment door, and fumbled with its crystal doorknob until it opened.

In her bedroom she could hear, as we always could hear, the hiss of oxygen. "Lynn," she said, her voice sounding strange in the quiet. "Lynn, we've got a problem." My grandfather woke, pulled on his slacks and stepped into his black shoes. She told him about the man in the lobby, and he opened his bureau and pulled out a sawed-off cue-stick. "All right," he said. "Let's go."

In the lobby, there was just enough light for them to identify the body. It was Forrest, the once-famous boxer. My grandfather squatted and shook his shoulder. "He's alive."

My grandmother exhaled. "Thank god for that."

"Forrest," he said. "Forrest!" He shook him harder, but Forrest barely budged. My grandfather looked up. "Go get a glass of water."

Stepping into the café, my grandmother returned with a tall water glass and handed it to my grandfather who then slugged the water in Forrest's face. This time, Forrest snorted, rolled over—facing the chandelier—and began to snore. My grandfather let out a half-chuckle, feeling both amused and sorry for the man. "Come on Forrest. *Forrest*—"

Nothing.

Finally my grandfather stood up clutching the pool cue and stepped to Forrest's feet.

"What're you doing?" Grandma asked.

"This will get him up."

He swung the pool cue striking Forrest hard across the bottoms of his shoes. Forrest sat bolt upright, his fists ready to go.

"Whoa, whoa, whoa!" my grandfather said, his hands in front of him defensively. "It's all right. It's all right. Let's just get you upstairs."

Forrest grumbled and rubbed his eyes. They helped him to his feet and walked him up the stairs, as if lugging an oversized rag doll. There was no judgment. They, too, had been there. They had lived in that bottomland, had bloodied each other, shattered dishes, driven cars off canyon roads, brandished knives, wielded threats, and had, worst of all, abandoned hope for themselves. So what ensued that morning among the three of them was a quietness that filled the space where words might have been spoken, but would have failed in their reach for meaning. No speeches, no apologies, no judgment. Just some light laughter in the twilight of morning, pats on the back, and help to a room.

11. Boom and Bust

I had just settled in and was beginning to see myself as a part of something larger and important. Then the walkout ended. We would go back to Washington over Thanksgiving break. "You'll start third grade there," my mother said.

I was devastated. I was doing well enough in school and the rift that had once existed between me and Mrs. Jones had been repaired, at least in my eyes. Most important, B.J. and I were best friends, and I couldn't bear the thought of uprooting once more, of abandoning that kind of trust. But we did, and before I knew it, I was again standing on the lawn in front of that paint-flecked clapboard house in the desert.

I hated everything about being back in Washington. I hated the too-small house itself, the neighbor kids, and third grade. Then one day I was pulled from my class and given a battery of tests. The tests indicated that I was "gifted," and within a week I was transferred out of my regular third grade class and into an "advanced" classroom environment that was taught by two teachers simultaneously. The students comprised a hybrid assembly of advanced third graders and fourth graders. I felt out of sorts. I didn't belong with the third graders or the fourth graders. But within the year, Dad was laid off for good, and my sense of placelessness would soon end.

We packed up everything we owned and again crossed Oregon's Blue Mountains to Soda Springs, Idaho. I sat in the back of our 1974 Plymouth Roadrunner pinned between our large color television set and the window. A U-Haul trailer wagged behind us while Dad sat coolly behind the wheel calling Ronald Reagan and the Republicans a syndicate of "cocksuckers," as we made this move from Washington to Idaho, from one desert to another. From Hanford to Monsanto.

When the landscape of Soda Springs swung into view and filled our windshield, I could hardly contain my excitement. Early summer in the high desert and the grasses were still green.

It was decided that I would return to my rollaway bed beneath the skylight in the living room of my grandparents' spacious apartment, while my mother and dad moved into a larger, corner apartment with a small kitchen with a speckled linoleum floor and appliances from the 1950s. Their living room was small and opened into their bedroom, and beyond the bedroom was the bathroom with a deep tub and a pull-chain light bulb. We bought a set of intercoms that would offer a volley of squawky dialogue between apartments.

Many changes had occurred in our absence. My grandparents bought a reddish Pomeranian-Dachshund puppy and named her Ribbons. B.J. had a baby sister. My grandfather's emphysema had worsened significantly. And the building had changed some, too. The lobby had new carpet and had been partitioned off into a banquet hall. The black and red checked tiles in the café had been covered with low-pile carpeting. And much of the lighting was new.

While Dad was happy to help my grandparents run the hotel, he must have resented—if only inwardly—the new arrangements. He put on the face of the amiable and eager helper, but deep inside, the one thing he feared—that oppressive sense of being landlocked or stuck in place—would have chewed away at him. He must have seen the Enders Hotel, a resting stop for wayward travelers—people with his drifter blood—as the end of his movement. It would have been impolite and ungrateful for him to have complained about the hotel and these new arrangements, so he channeled his frustrations and panic toward my mother and me specifically and the town itself in a more general sense. "That's life in Bugtussle, U.S.A.," he would say, his tone vacillating from playful mockery to derisiveness. I couldn't help but take it as a personal affront. After all, Soda Springs was my home. It was my place and if it promised permanence, I was only happy to abide.

Dad grew up on the move, and because the pattern of movement was the only constant thing in his childhood, he had come to trust it and rely on it, and to stake it out as his sole ally in whatever wars he was fighting. His wasn't a method of running away, but just running period. All the promises of good work existed in some distant sunset like a wash of coins in the sky. And onward he chased. As a boy growing up in the dusty reaches of Roosevelt, Utah, Bud Schrand used to pick rock or move sprinkler pipe for local farmers. Generally his brother Larry joined him—the Schrand boys out to make a wage. More than once, though, their stepfather, Dean—a jowly man with a paunch and flattop—worked with the boys on the same job. But that kind of arrangement always ended the same way—with the farmer finding Dean stumbling drunk in a dust-choked field, or passed out behind a livery, face down in the grass. Of course the boys would leave the job, too, their faces branded red with humiliation. "Pops is okay," they'd assure one another. "Just drinks too much."

Dad's grandmother grew up in Mexico but fled when she met a professional gambler who swept her north to Kansas City, Missouri. Dad's mother, Vivian, tells a famous story of her childhood spent in and around the gaming houses and back alleys of Kansas City and how she used to sit on Pretty Boy Floyd's lap. "He used to bounce me on his knee," she often recalls.

Eventually, the family moved to Aberdeen, Idaho, another dust-blown settlement which was then populated with squat, tarpaper homes and trailer houses. Larger farmhouses stood at the edges of town and peered from well-lit dormer windows toward the town's blinking lights. After Aberdeen, Dad moved to Wyoming for work and then Pocatello, Idaho, and eventually—after his divorce from his former wife and after leaving his two daughters—he found his way to Soda Springs where he met my mother.

My mother, on the other hand, maintained a slightly more complicated relationship with the town. She was no stranger to the pattern of fleeing and returning for she had been living out that pattern almost her entire life. As a girl she spent many of her summers in Jackson Hole, Wyoming, with her biological father—my grandfather George—and as soon as she turned eighteen, she bolted for Idaho Falls, a town over a hundred miles northwest of Soda Springs, the town where she would meet Jerry Imeson. It is true that she felt safe in Soda Springs, and has always felt safe there, but it was the people, she said, that she could do without. "Oh, Brandon," she would say, "there's a whole lot of people in this town who just think *their shit don't stink*. I was from the wrong side of the tracks."

By the time we returned, my grandmother had finally assembled a loyal staff of cooks, waitresses, maids, dishwashers, and bartenders, but the road getting there was long, the turnover high. A man named Don, for instance, styled himself a chef and was, as it turned out, a good grill cook—when he wasn't drinking. Several times during his shift, he would disappear into the Santo Club (as in Monsanto), the bar on the other side of the café, for a double shot of bourbon and a beer chaser. One day during the noon rush, my grandmother stepped into the kitchen only to find Don sweaty-haired and swaying over the hot grill. Just as he about passed out facedown on the grill, she snatched his wrist, and towed him back into the kitchen out of public view. "Stay here, goddamn it," she said and left. She had gone to the apartment to enlist my grandfather: "You hired the son of a bitch, and you're going to fire him."

And so he did.

But another replaced him, a cook named Joe. He was a balding man with a gin-blossomed nose who was known for a volatile and unpredictable temper. But he, too, was a good cook. And like Don before him, Joe was a terrible drunk. Instead of drinking daily, he would clean up for long stretches, but inevitably something would spark his temper, and he would go on benders for days at a time. When my grandmother confronted him after a second or third of such incidents, he fired back: "Well, good luck finding someone to replace me. The only other cook worth a shit in this country is Ruth Langston, and she wouldn't work in a place like this."

"You might want to tell her that because I just hired her," my grandmother said.

Ruth Langston was the size of a meat locker and wore a dome of gray hair. She was an all-business kind of woman who knew everything about running a kitchen, how to cater a large party, everything. When she showed up, she took charge. She was decisive and to me, intimidating—the grand matron.

If waitresses lost their jobs it generally involved their dipping into the cash register. In my family, there couldn't be a higher offense than stealing, particularly because my grandparents were so charitable. I don't know how frequently they lent money to their employees, or fattened their Christmas bonuses, but it was often.

Even as a young boy I could tell the good "help"—as we called them—from the bad. But I liked best the ones who would indulge me in afternoon conversations while I sat at the yellow counter picking over my lunch. If they were pretty, that helped—more so later than earlier. The same rule applied to the cooks.

I could spot the bad help easily as they allowed their emotions to surface on the job. If they had to put up with a difficult customer (and we had two or three regulars), everyone else paid for it. Or if they were a clock-watcher, they wouldn't last. Our best help stayed late if needed, arrived early on principle, and worked large banquets because of the tips. And they respected me, teased me, and cajoled me. Most of all, if they had a gripe about my family—of which I'm sure there were many—they were wise enough to keep it to themselves while I was around.

12. Boys

On those first summer days back, I loved nothing more than to pass an afternoon in the café, drinking a root beer float, and plugging quarters into the jukebox. Alabama's "Mountain Music" and Eddie Rabbitt's "I Love a Rainy Night" were among my favorites. Some of my fondest memories extend beyond the jukebox to the sounds of business. The rhythmic song of the cash register. The clatter and clink of dishes and silverware. Banter and gossip and laughter and talk turned this cacophony into an opera of the everyday. And the smells. Sputtering eggs, sizzling bacon, roasted meats, coffee. And how my grandmother's hands always smelled like chopped onions and celery and cigarette smoke. I came to count on these sounds and smells as they defined, in some small way, the parameters of my youth.

But it was books that defined and shaped and influenced me most. That summer, before I entered the fourth grade, I started reading *The Adventures of Huckleberry Finn*. I had already read *The Adventures of Tom Sawyer* and couldn't wait to get to the stories of his cohort.

During the summer the Enders Café catered a number of company picnics and family reunions, all of which called for enormous amounts of food: one hundred pounds of coleslaw; one hundred-fifty pounds of macaroni salad; two hundred pounds of potato salad. And all of it was made by hand, by a group of women in the basement who circled a large yellow prep table. Each of them worked reddened and sore fingers as they chopped onions, cabbage, celery, and hard-boiled eggs. They were strong, broad shouldered, and wizened in that pragmatic rural way, a manner that would invite a mud poultice for a bee sting or a swab of bourbon for a teething child. Ruth usually took charge of these large-scale operations hauling five-gallon buckets of salad from the basement up the stairs into the parking lot where they were loaded into pickup trucks.

And for their entertainment and my edification, I read *The Adventures of Huckleberry Finn* entirely *aloud* to that circle of women, those prep cooks, in the wide open café basement. When it was bright and hot outside and dim and cool in the basement, and as they worked through the hours, I sat on hundred-pound sacks of potatoes and read my book, breathing in the rich, dank, and earthy scents of soil and burlap. Page after page I read aloud. Much of the language stumped me in its contracted, colloquial nuances. Lines like, "crabapples aint ever good, and the p'simmons wouldn't be ripe for two or three months yet," would halt my reading. I knew what crab apples were, but not the other. "What's p'simmons?" I'd ask the group of women. "That's *persimmons*," one would say. "A fruit. Don't grow around here, though." It was a strange and exciting language and I was pleased to read it out loud. Often I would add some drawl to the dialogue for effect. The cooks would smile and nod and say, "He's good."

"He sure is."

Mostly I was pleased to have that kind of attention.

When I finished my reading for the day, I would run up the back staircase, taking the wooden plank stairs two at a time, and shove out into the bright afternoon. Downstairs, the story had ended, for the time being, but it lived on inside me. So powerful was the story of Huck Finn that I wanted to live the equivalent of that boyhood fantasy.

That is when I decided to go barefoot for the summer, or at least as often as I could, and where I could. That is when I began an inventory of my pockets' contents: jackknife (recovered from a dusty shelf in the hotel basement), string, marbles, matches, loose change. I read closely. Whatever Huck had, I would have, too. I rolled my pants up to my knees, and started out tender-footed across the hot, gravel parking lot trying to avoid the glinting shards of brown and green bottle glass that winked from the gray.

Soon enough, my feet toughened, and I found my way beyond the geyser and the cemetery, across the railroad tracks and into the sagebrush and juniper fields where Soda Creek meandered through, a steady gleaming stream. The water was clear and bright and cold, and I explored its every turn, its every eddy and pool. A day seldom passed when I wouldn't peel off my shirt and plunge into the water and allow myself to float supine, my face to the sky.

Eventually I desired, like Huck, to build a raft. I would float Soda Creek starting in town, following it all the way to its confluence into the Bear River at the western-most edge of Soda Springs.

For this endeavor, I would enlist the help of B.J.

I never told B.J. that I had read or was reading *The Adventures of Huckleberry Finn*, nor did I go barefoot when he was around. We didn't talk books. So I never brought it up. But all I had to do is say the word *raft*, and he was in.

We started with two wooden pallets. Cruising the alley behind the main street stores, we found a mess of them stacked behind Western Auto. Not-so stealthily, we each grabbed one and lugged them up the alley toward Geyser Park. Our covert, if not Byzantine course eventually led back to the clubhouse. If we were caught stealing pallets, they'd string us up. We just knew it.

Once we made it back to the fort, I fetched from the hotel basement's tool room a couple of claw hammers, a tin of nails, spool of wire, nylon rope, four lengths of two-by-four, and a handsaw. We were in business. First we lashed the two pallets together, end to end, with the rope and wire. To stabilize the craft, we ran a three-foot length of two-by-four down the center, nailing it in place. Then we constructed a mast that rose from its center some four feet high. On it I would affix a sail improvised out of a hotel bed sheet. As we hammered away, we schemed. "Shit, I'll bet no one's gone down Soda Creek before," B.J. said.

"Hell no. We'll be the first."

"It's going to be awesome."

"I know. And if we can make the raft better and better, maybe we can take it down the Bear."

"Totally."

"Could you imagine?"

"We could go all the way to Grace." About eight miles southwest of Soda Springs, Grace was the nearest town.

"Or Salt Lake."

"Yeah. And if we ever get into trouble and have to, like, leave, we could escape on our raft."

We stopped, wiped the sweat from our foreheads, and took a moment to admire our work. We still had a few chunks of two-by-four left and saw no need to let them go to waste. "I'm going to build a captain's chair," I said.

"Me, too."

"Cool."

Our chairs turned out to be little more than two hunks of wood nailed to the center support beam at opposite ends, but they satisfied us all the same.

The first problem we hadn't anticipated was moving the raft. It weighed nearly as much as a sack of potatoes by the time we were done. Transporting two pallets tethered together with a four-foot mast sticking out of its middle a half mile over rough terrain, would be nearly impossible. We managed to lift it and stumble about three clumsy feet before we crashed into a weed patch.

We each let out a laugh and stood, patting the dust from our jeans. "Now what?" I said.

"We could drag it."

"How?"

"With rope."

"Good idea. I'll go get some."

In a flash, I had returned with more nylon rope from the tool room.

Dragging the rickety craft proved only slightly easier than carrying it. We fastened two separate lines to the raft, tied each end around our waists, and trudged. About every four or five feet the raft would catch a rock and stop us dead with a jolt to our waists. By the time we made it to the banks of Soda Creek, our midsections were raw with rope burns, we were spent, and the raft had nearly fallen apart. But we were undeterred.

The deepest place I ever found in Soda Creek measured maybe six feet. The rest of the stream averaged three to four feet deep, and seven to ten feet wide. It was perfect for our raft. Giddy with thoughts of high adventure, we stripped off our shirts, and lugged the craft to the water's edge. I jumped in and pulled the raft from the weedy bank. B.J. followed. "You ready?" I said, smiling.

"Shit yeah."

"On three—" On the three count we hoisted our waterlogged bodies on to the raft and noticed immediately the tremendous errors in our engineering. We managed to get our knees on board, but when we attempted to stand, the raft plunged to the bottom of the creek like a slab of concrete. And there we stood, on our raft, chest deep in the creek, blinking in the sun. The mast peeked up above the water, the only evidence of the craft at all. We were both amused and hugely disappointed.

I plunged my head under water and pulled back up. I cleared the water from my eyes and spit. "Damn it."

B.J. slapped the water. "So much for an escape raft."

If we drew our legs closer to our torsos, the raft would lift from the floor of the creek, and would float, about six to twelve inches from the muddy bottom, and we could ride it more or less like a submerged surfboard. That was enough. For the day. It became our great challenge, to surf this contraption down a meandering creek through a cow pasture. As it turned out, we didn't get anywhere near the confluence with the Bear River, but we made it close to the railroad tracks where we abandoned ship. By the end of the afternoon, our backs were beet red, and riddled with horsefly and mosquito bites. And so we walked back through fields in wet jeans as water seeped from our sneakers with every muddied step. We were happy even in the face of such a defeat because, after all, it was never about the raft. It was about the creek and the water and the junipers, and the cow dung we kicked apart. It was about that place because it was ours, and I could sense this truth as we walked home toward dusk with Monsanto at our backs and their tractors dumping cauldrons of radioactive molten slag. That magmatic sludge washed the sky orange and I was glad to be home.

13. The Artist

The people who took a room in the Enders Hotel were part of an unending, recursive movement. They arrived at our lobby desk on the tides of boom and checked out in the droughts of bust. And almost all of them were men. One morning I saw such a man standing at the desk. He looked tough and wind-burnt. Western shirt and jeans. I stopped short to study him, searching his face for traces of my own. He turned and looked at me and winked, gave a "'day" and then whistled a tune to fill the quietness of the lobby. I had said hello and then passed into the café. *It wasn't him*, I thought as I touched my face. Not this time. But one day, I figured. One day my father will walk through those sunlit lobby doors, ring the bell, and order will be restored. I could count on it.

In the meantime I studied other guests like the one I came to call the artist. Her name was Maya and when I saw her I stared even though I had enough manners that told me not to. She was taking the stairs to her room. She looked down, saw me, smiled, and then vanished. My grandfather stood at the desk and worked a stubby pencil over some triplicate carbon paper. "Who was that?" I asked.

"Just a gal staying here awhile, helping out some."

I knew what that meant. We often put up drifters, people who couldn't afford to shuck out the few dollars for one of our rooms. We took these people in and allowed them to work for their room and board. There was plenty to do at the Enders Hotel. Others bartered for a bed and a hot plate of food. The safe in my grandfather's office contained the relics of such impromptu commerce: watches, pounds of watches; pistols, rings, a camera, lockets—the material offerings of desperation. His closet held other tokens of transience: a guitar, rifles, a banjo minus strings, the bygone things of waywardness.

My grandfather met Maya in an AA meeting.

Maya, I came to find out, had the same plaque hanging on the wall in her room upstairs.

Perhaps in her mid-thirties, Maya was an artist and recovering alcoholic. She was unlike anyone I had every seen. All the girls I knew wore their hair large like frozen storms. Maya, though, wore straight dark hair cropped at her sharp collarbone. Fair complexion, glasses, dark sweaters, and jeans. Her eyes were two buttons of watery turquoise, and I remember how she always worked a wadded tissue in her hand, how she always seemed sick.

Early in my fourth grade year, I won an art contest. I drew a jaguar—the cat, not the car, although the cat I drew came from a magazine advertising the car. The contest inspired some sort of false confidence in me, because weeks later, I was telling girls on the playground that I was a budding artist. Could I draw their picture? "Of course," I said.

I had watched Maya only a few days before she spoke to me. I noticed the paint on her fingers—grays, some white, blues, and spots of red—and splotches on her jeans. I'd see her in the café over coffee and a salad with a wide sketchpad before her on the checkered table cloth. A cigarette burned in the ashtray at her elbow. She caught me looking at her drawing one afternoon. I don't remember what she was sketching, but I do remember her asking me if I liked to draw. To which I nodded and told her that I won an art contest.

"Really?"

"Yeah. I drew a jaguar—the cat, not the car."

"You'll have to show me sometime." She smiled and took up her cigarette.

"I've got it over in the apartment."

"Anytime is great," she said. "I'm just here."

"Wow. Thanks."

Two days later I rapped on her room door, the crayoned likeness of a jaguar in hand. She opened the fire-opal-colored door slowly, and when her eyes alighted on me she let a smile escape. I eyed the mint-colored walls, Mission Oak dresser overcrowded with books and papers. Paintings hung on the wall around the sign bearing the serenity prayer. A mound of clothes filled a corner near the brass radiator that squatted beneath the window. It was a very bright room. And I'll never forget how it smelled, how it was sour and medicinal and herbal all at once.

She saw me staring at her paintings. I hadn't said anything more than hullo if, in fact, I said that much. She looked at me and then at her paintings. "See one you like?" she asked. I did see one I liked, or at least one that I thought was interesting. "That one," I said, pointing. "There. The black flower."

"Oh, the snapdragon?"

A correction of terms I noted: *snapdragon.*

"Yeah. The snapdragon. I've never seen a black flower before."

"Neither have I."

"So how come you painted one?"

"Because, well, because that's how I *felt* at the time."

I nodded and adjusted my expression so that it might evoke understanding or something akin to what we might call sophistication. My face, I'm sure, reflected none of those things. Confusion, maybe. Or constipation. But not understanding.

Maya stayed with us for maybe a month or so, and we exchanged pleasantries whenever we saw one another.

"My dad was a painter," I said once.

"No kidding?"

"Yep."

"Maybe that's where your talent comes from. You still drawing?"

"Oh, yeah. But mostly painting."

"That's wonderful."

"I have some of those paint by number pictures I got at the drugstore."

She smiled widely holding back, perhaps, a laugh. "Good. They'll get you started."

When B.J. had to do chores at his house, I would pass several afternoons with my brushes and paints and those chalky white boards with their faint blue lines and coded numbers. Mountain scenes with a cabin tucked into the foothills, a creek snaking through a meadow. A wolf among aspens. A sagging barn in a sea of field grass. I loved how the picture came together as if by magic, and I loved the rich, oily scents of the paints. I would display my works in the apartment for my family to admire. When it came to reading, art, and, later, music, my family offered nothing but encouragement and praise—no small thing for a family cut from our particular stock. Of course no one in my family expected me to construct a career out of these interests, and therein existed the clearest distinction between work and play, between the world of boys and that of men.

Nevertheless, when I felt more daring, I would cart my small paintings into the café and show them off to the waitresses and cooks and customers, the town. "You've got real talent, there, kiddo," Jan, one of my favorite waitresses would say. "I'm afraid I never could do that."

And when I was particularly pleased with my work, I packed them upstairs and knocked on the fire-opal door to show Maya. More often than not, I found her reading and snacking on celery sticks or crackers. She would comment on the colors and how she liked them, and I would beam.

"I'd say you're ready to branch out on your own," she'd say.

"What do you mean?"

"I think you're good enough to start painting your own pictures."

"Really?"

"Oh, sure."

Ecstatic with such an endorsement, I sprinted down the dim stairway taking the stairs by twos, and into the apartment where I started to work on my own paintings under the skylight. My materials were humble: watercolors and sheaves of notebook paper. I generally painted the things I knew, like the geyser, my clubhouse, the hotel, or a girl at school.

Once when my mother stopped in the apartment to visit with me and take a smoke break, I told her about Maya's encouragement. "So that's why I'm doing my own now."

"I think you should," she agreed. "But I also think you need to leave Maya alone, Brandon."

"How come?"

"Because."

"Because why?"

"Just because."

"Did she do something or something?"

"No. You just don't need to be bothering her. That's all."

I was wounded. It was the same story. Stay away from the people upstairs.

Every now and then I would see Maya and give a hullo or a wave and she would pause a moment in the lobby, find a tentative smile, say hi, and continue on. At one point I wondered if Maya had also been told not to bother me.

But I kept painting. Moving from the paint by number medium, I decided to begin in oils which I had also purchased at the drugstore. But I was often careless with my things and had left the cap off the red paint for an entire day and when I returned to my painting, it was dry and cracked like a desert floor. I added some water, but it just turned into clumps. So I dumped it into the toilet, and for whatever reason, did not flush. A few hours later, my grandfather stepped into my room and looked pale, stricken. "Brandon, did you put anything in the toilet?"

"Yeah. I dumped my red paint in there. Is it clogged or something?"

He laughed and leaned against the wall in relief. "Thank God. I thought something might have been wrong with your grandma," he said. "That it was blood."

Maya's legacy endured for years after she checked out of the Enders Hotel. It was a small thing, really, but one I thought of often. Like so many others who boarded with us, Maya worked for her room and meals. Whenever possible, my grandfather drew on her skills as an artist. So one Sunday when our family was busy shampooing carpets, mopping, cutting meat, and all of the other chores that came on the one day we were closed, Maya set up her easel at the front door of the café. Her job was simple, but to Grandpa's way of thinking, necessary. "We need a 'Pull' sign on this door," he had instructed her. "So our customers quit trying to push their way out." The glass door was held in place by a thick, brushed aluminum frame, and on its edge, Maya painted the word "pull" in black capitals that fell in a column. It was a command: *PULL*. And every time I slipped out of the café to amble down the sidewalk to Eastman Drug or sprint across the street for a movie at the Idanha, I paused if for only an instant and considered the word and the woman who put it there. I would never forget those black letters or her black hair cropped at her collarbone, or that singular black snapdragon.

14. The Texans

Some people checked in to the Enders to drink, others, like Maya, checked in to quit. And some arrived simply because they had no other place to go. The Texans, for instance, arrived because we were the only option. Autumn replaced summer, and aspen leaves fell to the streets like a million harvest moons pasted on a wash of night. Wood smoke scented the air. The distant thud of hunters' rifle fire echoed from Eight Mile Pass and Trail Canyon. During this time my grandfather's condition was worsening, it seemed, by the hour.

It was a Saturday when they arrived, and for me that meant stock day in the café. One of my earliest jobs was to fill the supply cupboards with all the canned goods the cooks would use in the week's time. I loaded gallon cans of pickles, whole tomatoes, corn, green beans, and chow mein noodles on to an expansive and deep set of shelves in the back of the kitchen. When I was finished, and the generic labels faced me neatly all in a row, I hauled empty cardboard cartons out to the dumpsters in the parking lot.

That's when I saw their 1960s blue and rusted International Travelall jalopy lurching into our parking lot, top-heavy with bundles and bags and cases strapped to its roof. One of the back windows had been blown out, evidently, and a sheet of transparent plastic took its place and was duct-taped at the edges. I noticed the mismatched tires—one knobby, one studded, the other two bald—and the dents in the fenders and the door panels. A youngish man perhaps in his thirties sat behind the wheel. His hair was long, unkempt, and fell to his shoulders in a shock like field straw. His wife sat at his elbow in the passenger seat. I could see her hair was long and dark and stringy. She held something in her lap that I couldn't make out, but would later learn was a baby. A mess of kids filled the back, and I could see them pressing their bony faces to the windows. Palms flattened out against the jalopy's glass, and patches of foggy breath expanded and contracted on the panes.

A cool breeze worked at my shirt and the sun was warm on my back as I pitched the boxes into the black, large-bellied garbage cans. When I turned to head back into the hotel, I heard the creak and moan of the car door opening. I stopped and glanced back. The man who unfolded his lanky frame from the cab of the Travelall did so tentatively. "Excuse me," he said. "Do you know a—" He paused as he read from a blue slip of paper, and then said, clearly and carefully, "Lynn Beus?" The scrap of paper had no doubt led him and his family here.

"He's my grandpa," I said.

"Know where I might find him?" He stuffed the piece of paper into his shirt pocket. The kids in the back made a stir and the man looked back and hushed them.

"He's inside," I said. "I'll go get him."

"Appreciate that," he said.

My grandparents' large bedroom window looked out on to the parking lot and the geyser beyond that. They had bought separate beds when Grandpa started having trouble breathing, when he was first diagnosed with emphysema, and his bed sat closest to the window.

Through the opaque windowpanes in his arched bedroom door, I could make out the blurred image of my grandfather sitting on his bed. How often did I see not the members of my family, but their obscured shadowy figures through glass? How often would I watch them through the French doors as they approached the apartment from the lobby, their distorted figures coming into focus, their bodies shrinking to hard, discernible lines? It must have been hundreds or thousands, perhaps. I knocked softly, and turned the crystal doorknob. "Grandpa?" I said.

"Hey, Brat," he said and took off his horn-rimmed reading glasses.

"Grandpa, there's some people out there—"

"Okay." He'd watched them pull up, and knew even without my saying it, that he had been called on.

My grandfather kept a small TV tray near his bed strewn with any number of books and newspapers, a round tin of chewing tobacco, his glasses, a spit can, pens, a pad of paper, and generally, a bowl of fruit. I walked over and helped myself to a handful of black cherries. I'd seen a crate of them on the kitchen counter when I came in. "Don't eat too many of those," he cautioned. "You'll be shitting through a keyhole at fifty yards."

I laughed and said I wouldn't. I swallowed the dark red meat of a cherry and spit its stone into my grandfather's waste basket. He pulled out a comb from his trouser pocket, ran it through his graying hair, shoved it back into his pocket, and slipped on his black loafers. Today he hadn't needed his oxygen as much. Today was a good day, one of the rare ones.

He crossed the parking lot in the yellow light, and shook hands with the man. I stayed back and peeked through a crack in my grandparents' back doorway. I understood to stay away from these kinds of conversations—not because I wasn't allowed to know what was being discussed or arranged, but because it was impolite. No one wanted a kid hanging around when they needed to ask for money, work, or food. And people asked often enough that I knew this, whether or not the rule had actually been uttered out loud or not. Not unlike the American West itself, the Enders Hotel was a world of tacit understandings.

That afternoon, I spotted my grandfather sitting at the counter in the café over a bowl of oyster stew, a vile dish in my mind what with those gray bodies floating in hot milk and slicked with melted butter. His shirt sleeves were rolled to the middle of his forearms and a folded newspaper lay at his elbow. I straddled the stool beside him. "So who were those people?" I asked.

He scanned his paper and dabbed the corner of his mouth with a napkin and said, "Just a family that's fallen on some hard times."

"What do you mean?"

"Just that they're having a hard time making ends meet, finding a job, that sort of thing."

"You mean they're *poor*?"

"I don't know about *that*. They're not as well-off as you or me."

"They look kinda poor," I said.

"And they probably think *you* look like a brat, Brat," he said and winked.

I spun around on the stool, paused, and then said, "Where they from?"

"He said Texas."

"Huh," I said trying to picture what Texas might be like. "How long will they be here?"

"Not long."

"How long is that?"

"Long enough to do a little work around here."

"Oh," I said.

"How big are the kids?"

"Probably a little younger than you."

I nodded. I knew what that meant. *Probably too young for you. Let them be.*

My grandfather was a master of the understatement. The hard

truth is that the family bound for Texas was flat broke and hungry, and they had a baby. On the outskirts of town they had been pulled over for a broken taillight and expired plates. The man told the police officer he was looking for some short-term work to help finance their way home, and the police officer said to check with Lynn Beus over at the Enders Hotel. "It's the biggest building on Main Street," he would have told him. "You can't miss it."

This happened all the time.

Once when I was too young to notice or remember, the police called my grandfather and said they had picked up "quite a group" and asked if he could put them up. Quite a group turned out to be seventeen people—six adults and eleven children. Each one was bone-frail, ragged, and dirty. They were given rooms, beds, fresh towels, and were shown the community bathrooms at the ends of each hallway. When they cleaned up, my grandfather had told them, they could get some dinner in the café downstairs. They skipped the offer to wash or bathe, but cashed in on the dinner, a fact that doesn't escape my grandmother. "They didn't even *bathe*," she says with an evident amount of disgust. "And they didn't offer to work in return either. Nothing, not even a 'thank you.'" When the group left in the thin hours of dawn, they stole blankets, bed sheets, towels, soap, pillows, and "god knows what all," my grandmother adds when telling the story.

The County generally gave my grandparents a small amount of money to help compensate, but it was seldom, if ever, enough to cover everything—especially if items had gone missing. But my grandparents weren't looking for a money maker, and they didn't take people in so they could break even. They took people in because it was, to their way of thinking, the right thing to do.

I often think of the numbers of broken people who came to us during those years, and of those who simply had no other place to go. And that ours wasn't so much a dead end, but a place that spelled out the end of things, even if that end wasn't clearly in sight. More often than not you could guess the inevitable fall that our boarders would take once they left—their last breath, chance, misstep, the rattling whisper of things to come, an utterance as clear as the final rustle of those aspen leaves before the snows. The Hitchhikers. Ex-cons. Addicts. Drifters. Hustlers. Or the occasional rarity, like the square-jawed Amish boy who stayed with us for a number of weeks, who worked in his shirtsleeves and hat, thankful, it seemed, to earn a few dollars so he could get home. Or the old man who arrived on foot, bent like a stick, awash in liver spots, with wispy hair, a tattered satchel, and a bedroll, who paid his way with Morgan silver dollars—the ones with the reeded edge and Lady Liberty, dating from the 1880s. One dollar for a plate of food and room for the night. He was quiet, watery-eyed, and gave a gummy smile when our waitresses served him coffee or hot biscuits or a sandwich.

But it was even rarer that we took in an entire family like the Texans. For some reason, their arrival threw the world into sharp relief. One family quietly took in another and I was asked, as always, not to bother them. Pretend they weren't even there.

Something else from that time. My grandfather's disease. If he smoked before he volunteered for service in World War II, he smoked twice as much by the end of the war. There is little doubt that smoking caused his disease. But for years after the war, his lungs saw no reprieve. He harvested grain on combines without cab enclosures, mowing through fields in a whorl of splintery chaff and dust. And when he wasn't working on the ranch, he clocked time at Monsanto, where stacks of smoke and fire blasted from the mine's columns day and night. The amount of energy it takes to run the plant's furnaces for a single day could power all of Kansas City, Missouri, for the same twenty-four-hour period. Locals talk about this fact as if it is something to brag about. For seven years, my grandfather worked at Monsanto. That was in the late 1950s. It was, in many ways, a new time that promised greater things to come. Monsanto set up shop then with a single furnace, and a hundred or so employees bustled about the industrial complex. Now an industry of multiple furnaces, Monsanto is the chief employer and Soda Springs is, whether people say it aloud or not, a company town.

Crowded around the perimeter of the plant are a number of secondary and tertiary processing plants and facilities, each of them subordinate to the main. When Monsanto shuts down, and it will eventually, like all extractive industries, the outlaying companies will fold along with it. One collapse will follow the next and a majority of the people in this town will be forced to load their suitcases into their vehicles and move away looking for new promises. And those age old patterns of Western movement will resume. Not unlike the Texans, or my own family, for that matter, these people will load up and try to find their way to safety.

Head bowed as if in walking prayer, and with his hair swishing to and fro, the man bound for Texas seemed polite and his eyes cast a reticent, if plaintive, gaze. On the evening of their arrival, the man from Texas was busy getting his family settled in, squaring away the extra rollaway beds my grandfather had furnished them. It wasn't long before my curiosity outgrew my family's orders to avoid the Texans, and within a few hours, I darted up two flights of stairs under the guise of looking for my grandfather. What I wanted to see, clearly, were the children, to see if they wanted to play or hang out. To see if they wanted me to show them around. At first I saw only the skinny father in his fray-thin jeans and flannel over-shirt with his elbows sticking through holes. He had been lugging their belongings up the stairs to the second floor, to their room. But then, when I turned down the next hallway, I saw a white-haired boy of maybe four or five years step out from the community bathroom at the end of the hall. The bathroom had a high window and light green walls and a tall door that framed his small body. His hair was a mess and he was clutching what appeared to be a tattered swatch of blanket. I stopped and caught my breath as we made eye contact. For an instant it appeared as if he was afraid, as if he might cry or bolt or scream. "Hello," I said softly. "You staying here?"

He nodded and pointed down the hall behind me toward his room.

"That's nice. Me, too. But downstairs."

He stared at me as if waiting for me to say something more, but I did not know what else I might say, so I said, "Well, I better go."

On my way back to the stairs, a door opened and the young woman stepped out holding her baby. She was smaller than I had imagined and offered a faint and—what, exactly? Apologetic? Reluctant?—smile, and called to her boy down the hallway. I smiled back and vanished down the staircase into the openness of the hotel lobby.

My grandfather had checked them into room 130, the largest. I called it The Suite. It felt satisfying to think we owned a hotel that featured a suite even though my conception of a suite was vague. On their room door, just above the brass room number, one could make out the faint lettering: "Ladies' Parlor." I didn't know what a ladies' parlor was then, but I imagined it would have been something extravagant. I imagined pretty women preening before large, oval mirrors. Ornate furnishings and elevated, cultured language. I could see these women reading from literary volumes I had never heard of. I imagined a lifestyle so rich and delicate that it could be shattered by the slightest misstep, too much light or darkness, a careless word or phrase—a world, in other words, that could not have possibly inhabited the Enders Hotel as I knew it. Still, I saw things in that dream that belonged only to the leisured class. But the family that had just checked into this room, the suite, the parlor that had shed its opulence like a veil, was not of that class. There was nothing extravagant about this family.

Only when I realized that my family was keeping me from encountering the Texans just as much as they were withholding their own children from me or us or *this,* did I give up and shuffle into the café for dinner. But even then, I hadn't given up completely.

So I hovered over my dinner longer than usual. Once I finished my Swiss steak, canned green beans, and mashed potatoes, I walked behind the counter and poured some more soda into my cup from the fountain. I dumped my plate in the gray dish-tub, and asked Becky, our night waitress, for a slice of pie.

"What's it going to be?"

"Chocolate mousse," I said.

"I figured," she said and laughed. She grabbed the saucer from the pie case, and set it before me. I looked around but did not see any trace of the family bound for Texas. Business was slow. My mother was in the back of the kitchen prepping for the next day's menu. My grandmother was in the apartment taking a short break before closing. Dad was in the walk-in cutting rib-eye steaks for the week. At the back of the hotel sat a cinderblock building we called the "walk-in." It was our own slaughterhouse, and inside, a large, white, wooden walk-in cooler took up the majority of the room in the building. Two freezers, a long cutting table, butcher block, band-saw, grinder, and an old gas stove took up the rest of the space. A large meat-cuber sat on the long cutting table, smiling its rows of stainless-steel teeth. And above it, taped to the white cinderblock wall, hung a poster of a cow diagrammed into steaks, roasts, tenderloins, stew meat, filets, and cutlets. The walk-in itself, insulated with a ten-inch-thick wooden door, contained quarter sides of beef that swung from meat hooks while threads of blood drained from the marbled flanks and congealed on swatches of cardboard below. We threw scraps of fat, sinew, and meat that had fallen to the floor out to the alley cats. In the winter the meat reddened the snow and a litter of cats would crowd around it alternating their purrs with furtive, territorial hisses, like the meat was fresh, like it had been their kill.

And my grandfather, no doubt, was sitting on the edge of his bed, watching the sun slip into the west. He was getting some air. Tubes ran into his nose. And he sat there staring out his bedroom window into the parking lot. I am sure he would have finished his bowl of black cherries by then, spitting the last of the stones into the yellow wastebasket at his ankles. I knew where everyone in my family was and what they were doing, but the Texans were nowhere to be seen.

I finished my pie, placed the saucer on top of my dinner plate in the dish-tub, and started to leave when I stopped and turned to Becky. "Hey," I said. "The family that's staying upstairs—did they come down and eat yet?"

"He did," she said. She was refilling ketchup bottles. "I mean, he came down and got some orders to go, and took them upstairs. Why?"

"Just curious," I said and shrugged. I turned toward the door that connected the lobby with the café and started to leave.

"He seems real nice," she added. "Quiet, but nice."

"Yeah," I agreed and paused for a beat. "Well, see ya."

"Have a good night, Brandon."

"You, too."

I crossed the lobby, passed the large desk trailing my index finger across its dark, polished wooden edge, and opened the French doors to the apartment. Grandma sat in her recliner with her feet up. She was reading a mystery novel. A Bel-Air Menthol cigarette burned in an ashtray on an end table at her elbow. I was always drawn to the artwork that adorned her cigarette packages: a picture of crisp, blue windblown skies with a light cloud. Each package came with a coupon which, in number, could be redeemed for merchandise from the company's catalog. She collected the coupons, stowing them in a shoebox to give to me. I would spend hours leafing through the Raleigh-Bel-Air catalog dreaming of all the stuff I could get: compasses, watches, binoculars, bicycles, skateboards, sleeping bags, microscopes, anything. Eventually, I circled with blue ink a red telescope and a two-man inflatable raft—a raft that would finally take B.J. and me down Soda Creek and into the Bear River. But I needed more coupons.

I stepped through the apartment and out the back door. Outside, the sun was gone. It was dark and I shook off a chill. To the north, a Monsanto pot carrier had just dumped its molten slag and everything for miles burned orange. And for a few minutes, the night was light again. I stared at the battered Travelall in the parking lot. And I turned to look toward my grandfather's bedroom window. His lamp was on and I could see him sitting on the edge of his bed in his white T-shirt and tan trousers. I knew we were looking at the same thing. The Travelall that squatted in the parking lot. To me it was one of the most forlorn and resigned sights I had ever seen. That shell of bolts and rubber and parts signified another world, and I was looking right at it, dead on, illuminated.

The next day after school, I had dumped my backpack in my bedroom, and opened the apartment door to head over to the café when I almost ran right into the thin man from Texas.

"Sorry," I said, startled.

"My fault," he said. "Wasn't watching where I was going." He smiled sheepishly.

Two white, fifty-pound bags of rock salt hung over each of his shoulders. We used this salt to condition the hotel water, to soften it. And he was carrying the softener salt down the basement stairs to the hotel's large conditioner that stood near the furnace room. This would become my job later on, when I could manage fifty-pound bags without injuring myself. But for now, it had been given to the man from Texas. He disappeared down the stairs and I headed for the café.

In the center of the lobby, though, I stopped and looked up at the large ceiling. I listened. All I could hear was some banter from the bar, the croon of the jukebox, the crack of billiard balls, the sounds I always heard. From the café I could hear dishes clinking and laughter. But I heard nothing from upstairs.

That night I lay in bed beneath the skylight in my room, and listened to the thrum of autumn rain on the panes above. I watched the downpour make shadows and patterns as it cascaded down the glass. But these patterns and shadows never found definition like those I caught in our arched doorways, and no two patterns were alike. It was just the rain and the ambient street light that colored it in shades of gray and green and black. I couldn't sleep for the image of that boy framed in the tall doorway swam across my every thought. He looked just like his father. They were like twins mismatched in size. Nor could I shake the look the boy gave me. That doleful, wanting look.

That night I tried to make sense of what their lives must be like, but my conception of their world still felt abstract. Although they were sleeping upstairs, and were eating the same food I ate, they seemed strangely absent, like they were standing at the edges. Or it was like they had taken vows of silence when they walked into our lives, bathed in our waters, drank from our cups, and breathed behind our doors. I wanted to hear a sign of life coming from their room. A laugh or sneeze, the patter of that boy's feet across our floor or down the hallway. I wanted to hear a door click shut, the gush of water from a faucet, or the rhythmic creak of bedsprings and the delicate moans that would follow.

Instead, I heard nothing under the skylight but the drumming of rain. And as I lay in my bed with my hands clasped behind my neck, I stared upward. And just before I drifted off to sleep I saw the skylight turn orange and I heard my grandfather wheeze in the next room.

Like Maya before them, and so many people before her, the Texans left quietly on an early morning as the building slowly filled with light. My grandfather checked them out of their room, wished them luck, and gave them a handsome amount of cash to travel on. In the following weeks I would begin to wonder what our lives would be like without my grandfather. I began to consider his disease and its worsening effects, the fluid that drained from his eyes, that labored wheeze, the increasing time he spent on oxygen. But in the end, it was too much to think about. It was too abstract. It was easier to think about simpler things like a black snapdragon or a place called Texas.

15. The Knock of Experience

Late in the fall and well after the Texans left, a new kid showed up in my fourth grade class. His name was Sherrod and he wore longish, curly brown hair, a blue Yankees windbreaker (always), and had just moved from Las Vegas where his mother—or so it was whispered scandalously at the café—worked as a *cocktail waitress*, a term I took to mean *hooker*. This image was vaguely exciting in its explicitness, and conjured in my imagination floating snapshots of red satin and a fury of lights and flesh, but beyond those tinseled dreams, the image blurred.

What I liked about Sherrod was that he lived in an apartment above Gagon's Hardware (pronounced *jay-guns*) with his dad—a Monsanto engineer and closet poet. As far as I knew he and I were the only kids in my entire school who lived in apartments. Save the privileged few who lived in large houses on the edge of town called the Cedar View, everyone else lived either in postwar homes, trailers, or ramblers north of town in the Finlayson Subdivision. Not long before Sherrod arrived, a girl in my class—one I thought was cute for her blonde hair—laughed when I told her I lived at the Enders. "You live in a *hotel room*?"

"No, I live in an apartment."

"*Ewww*," she said, wrinkling her nose. And in one drill-team-like motion, she tossed her hair and made a dramatic, self-important exit.

"We own it," I tried even as she marched off, but the information was lost in the widening space between us. I felt winded, gut-punched. A distinction had been drawn and its line was steadily becoming more and more clear to me. In this way, Sherrod was an instant ally. But there was one more thing. Sherrod had attended Catholic school in Las Vegas, a fact I associated not with religion so much as wealth, confusing it, perhaps, with prep school. Although he was not a practicing Catholic, he was never without his St. Christopher's necklace. On the other hand, I was utterly without formal religion. In Washington I had ridden a white school bus to a Baptist church every Sunday while my mother and dad nursed their hangovers, but that was the extent of my exposure to theology. Two things explain the character and cultural makeup of Soda Springs, Idaho: Monsanto and Mormonism. It's a company town with a peculiar stripe of piety. And in Soda Springs, belonging to both of these orders meant something, which I sensed.

I had but the faintest idea that my own family could trace its roots in the muddy history of the Mormon Church, and would learn years later just how deep my blood ran into the polygamous corridors of that complex American religion. I asked several times about this lineage, desperate to nail down a recorded history, something official on which I could drop anchor. But the answers were even more clipped and abbreviated than those I heard when I asked about my father, Jerry Imeson. (When I did learn of this past, I was shocked by many things, and how it all led to me. How, for instance, my great-great-grandfather, William McClellan, fought in the Mormon Battalion—the only religious detachment in the Civil War—was a Colonel in the Nauvoo Legion, the Mormon Church's own paramilitary operation, established a polygamous colony in Colonia Juarez, Mexico, beat his children mercilessly, took three wives one of whom vanished without a trace, dodged federal marshals all his life, may have been involved in, or had knowledge of, the Mountain Meadows Massacre, and died alone a wanted man in Mexico while the rest of his family left him in his grave, and loaded their wagons for Utah. But none of this was discussed in my family. It was one of those closed chapters to which they did not return for reasons that had less to do with shame or denial, and more to do with the dull and broad axe of time that cut them off from their past. They had too much to attend to in the present to be sidetracked by what lurked in the twilight of yesteryear. What I learned came slowly, through my own storm of questions and my growing impatience for half-stories. I needed to know what I had inherited and from whom I had inherited it.)

So Sherrod, the wayward Catholic, fell in easily with B.J. and me. If B.J.'s family was Mormon it was only official or documentary and never in practice. But at the time, church merely signified whether or not one had Sundays off. B.J., Sherrod, and I had our Sundays to ourselves, and slowly, wonderfully, that's when our trouble began.

That Sherrod seemed to possess a worldly knowledge I could never reach, never even touch, redoubled his post as friend, confidant, and ally. He told wild stories of Las Vegas and of cruising the Strip on his bike, finding cash, dodging seedy characters, and darting through the sketchy neighborhoods of North Las Vegas. He had smoked his first cigarette in Las Vegas, sipped from his first beer, and learned the ways and rhythms of a world so foreign to me that, when spun, his stories cast a spell as alluring as the silver screen itself.

B.J. and I had tried cigarettes and beer by the fourth grade. (But not in Las Vegas—and that seemed to be the narrative element that made Sherrod's stories most appealing.) Once, for instance, while I was in Washington, B.J. had walked into the Maverick convenience store and asked the clerk for a paper sack even though he had not yet purchased anything. Reluctantly, the clerk gave him the sack, and watched with astonishment as the eight-year-old slipped behind the counter, dropped a carton of Marlboro Reds into the bag, and bolted out the front door and across the puddled parking lot. Her phone call to B.J.'s dad beat him home, and by the time B.J. arrived, breathless, guilty, and clutching his contraband, the gruff, axle-greased Beaver Weaver was awaiting his son's arrival on the front porch. The punishment was of the old school variety, something that today would land a parent behind bars, but at the time seemed to fit the crime: Beaver made B.J. sit on their crumbling cement porch of their clapboard home and smoke the entire carton of cigarettes.

My own brush with smoking and drinking occurred in Washington and came by way of the rollicking parties my parents threw to the sultry romp of Credence Clearwater Revival. While the parents passed around joints, listened to records, and laughed, a few of us kids absconded with beers and pilfered smokes into a grove of cherry trees behind the house.

My family adored B.J. and called him one of their own. I enjoyed, too, the same privileged treatment in his home. As it turned out, though, this wasn't the case with Sherrod. My mother liked Sherrod well enough, but my grandmother had her reservations. Even at a young age, Sherrod exuded an air of smugness that didn't square with her no-nonsense view of the world. Despite her work-a-day, field and plough background, and her frankness, my grandmother could act strangely Victorian, and it was her attention to manners and social behavior that pitted her against Sherrod's wink-and-smile finesse.

Sherrod's father never extended a terribly warm welcome to either me or B.J. and had devised a fortress of rules that kept us at bay: usually out on the front sidewalk in front of Gagon's Hardware where we waited for Sherrod, shivering with our hands jammed into our jeans pockets.

I will always remember my fourth grade year, that entire era. That fall I had turned ten, and was beginning to develop a sense of myself. It's a fascinating age. You begin to cast your small shadow of autonomy over your family. You no longer accept the world on its face, and delight, even, in rejecting orders or ideas that your parents hand down. Or at least I did. That year I learned Idaho history—a strange thing to remember, really, but I was enthralled with the stories of mountain men, trappers, Indians, traders, and pioneers. I learned all the state emblems, and committed to memory the state bird: Mountain Bluebird; the state horse: Appaloosa; the state flower: Syringa; the state motto: Esto Perpetua. *We are the Gem State, not the Potato State*, I would say piously to an imaginary audience as if correcting the world's perception in one single, sweeping breath.

It was also the year B.J., Sherrod, and I started hanging out in the clubhouse every day after school where we smoked yellowed lawn grass rolled in newspaper in the hopes that it might give us a high, but experienced instead a sharp fertilized burn straight to our lungs. Only after we determined that the grass wasn't working like we imagined it should, did I start stealing boxes of Lipton Decaffeinated Tea from the café basement. One day I broke open over a dozen bags and dumped the greenish tea into a sandwich bag, mimicking what I had seen at so many of my parents' parties in Washington. When B.J. and Sherrod came over they ogled the baggie: "Is that the real shit?"

"Yeah."

"No way."

"Smell it."

They each leaned forward and drew a full breath. Sherrod was the first to call bullshit. "What is it? Because it's not weed."

"It's tea," I confessed. "I took it from the basement."

"Won't your folks notice?" B.J. asked.

"No one drinks it. It's decaf. I stock all the cupboards and I've never had to stock this stuff. It just sits there."

"It looks real," B.J. said, grabbing the baggie.

"We could sell it as the real thing. Most people wouldn't even know," Sherrod said, snatching it from B.J.

"You think?" I asked.

"Totally. Half the shit that's sold in Vegas is fake. But people still buy it." Sherrod buried his nose in the baggie and sniffed.

"What if we get busted?" I asked.

Sherrod looked up and scoffed. "For what? Selling tea? That's why it's *perfect*. They can't do anything to us."

B.J. laughed. "Yeah, but who's going to buy it?"

"The sixth and seventh graders. High schoolers would know the difference."

"Cool," I said, thinking it over.

"Have you tried it, though?" Sherrod asked.

I shook my head.

"Let's give it a try!"

"We're out of newspapers."

Sherrod picked up a pop can from the corner of the clubhouse and shook out the remaining few drops of cola. "Don't need any."

We watched as Sherrod transformed a regular pop can into a pipe by denting its center, and filling the dent with tiny nail holes. He jabbed one more hole into the side of the can and held it up. "The best part," he said, eyeing his improvised paraphernalia, "is that when you're done, you just smash it and throw it away."

I pinched a wad of the green tea and loaded it into the bowl on the pop can. I struck a match from a book that read THE ENDERS HOTEL, CAFÉ & LOUNGE 208-547-4980, touched the yellow flame to the tea, and inhaled. It was less harsh than the fertilized schoolyard grass, and this, we thought, was a small victory.

What a strange and insular life boyhood is. It is comprised of its own rules and codes and language, something that feels like the sum of existence at the time (and it *is*), and yet is increasingly difficult to access through the distance of so many years. But distance gathers like night, and memory flickers proportionately. Knowing I cannot go back, truly, but that I can look back, offers both comfort and disquietude in equal helpings. It is in the casting back, the remembering, and the sifting through stories that I try to break the integument of that wholly insular world and see it for what it was: not childhood masquerading as childhood, but boys standing in the shadows of their fathers; boys rapping at the door of experience.

One afternoon of that year there came such a rap on the door of the clubhouse. B.J., Sherrod, and I were puffing away on another pop can filled with smoldering tea. The knock itself came as a shock and jolted us from our haze and sour stomachs. We fanned the air hopelessly, knowing, somehow that we weren't eliminating the smoke so much as rearranging it.

I peered through a hole between two large stones in the wall and spotted my cousin, Vince, dancing nervously outside, looking here and there as if someone were tailing him.

"It's Vince," I said. A calm fell over the dank and dark quarters of the stone fort, and I unlatched the lock and let him in.

The son of my mother's sister, LaNae, Vince was two years older than I was, easy going, albeit affected, and, unlike anyone in our Scottish-Irish family, had the enviable darker skin of his Polynesian father. As if adhering to a larger, generational family pattern, his parents divorced about as soon as they were married, leaving LaNae alone to fend for Vince and his older sister, Andrea. But during that year, Vince, who was in the sixth grade, lived across town with his dad—a man I admired because he resembled Rocky Balboa, had webbed feet, and drove a mint condition '56 Chevy.

Vince stepped into the smoky den and laughed. "What the hell have you guys been smoking?" His dark hair was long and feathered and fell to his shoulders brushing the straps on his turquoise tank top.

"You know," I said casually, and smirked. "A little weed."

Vince motioned for the pop can and B.J. handed it to him. "I hope you didn't *buy* this shit, because it ain't what you think it is."

His deft observation essentially dispelled our hopes to sell to

95

the sixth grade market, and we were forced to tell him that it was tea—*decaf*.

"Oh, that's a good one. That's *good*. Decaf!" He laughed it up while we looked down feeling miserable in our childishness. "It'll probably make you go sterile."

"What's that mean?" I asked.

"Means you can't have kids, dip-shit."

It was a strange threat to level against a ten-year-old, but it filled me with dread and confusion all the same. Part of me knew, too, that it wasn't true, that it couldn't be true. Besides what did Vince know about *that*?

"You guys want to see the real shit?"

We all leaned forward while Vince pulled his own baggie from his jeans pocket. "Check *this* out."

"What is that, about an eighth?" Sherrod asked.

Vince looked at him, surprised, perhaps by Sherrod's invocation of the proper nomenclature. It was, in fact, a term I had heard but never registered, never tried out for myself: *an eighth*.

"Yeah. About that. It's good shit."

"Where'd you get it?" B.J. asked.

"Wouldn't *you* like to know." Vince unrolled the bag and stuck his nose in it and breathed deeply. "Tell me that don't smell tits."

One by one we took the bag and put our noses in and huffed in the scent of the stenchy weed, nodding in agreement.

"Listen," Vince said. "I need to stash this here until things blow over a little."

"What do you mean?"

"I mean until things blow over, that's all."

"Like what kind of things," I pressed.

"Let's just say that I *borrowed* this and I need to ditch it for awhile. Somewhere safe. Like here."

"That's cool."

"But don't you touch it or I'll have your ass."

"I won't touch it," I said.

"We should at least get some of it," Sherrod said. "For keeping it here. I mean, what if we get caught with it?"

This had never occurred to me and it further proved my theory about Sherrod knowing things utterly unknowable to me.

"One bud," Vince agreed. "But no more."

The next day was a Friday and it was decided that Sherrod would stay over. After school, Sherrod came home with me to the Enders Hotel where we hung out in the clubhouse, goofed around on the geyser, and ate dinner in the café. That night we caught a movie across the street. The movie showing that night was *Gandhi*.

Once in the stony recesses of the clubhouse, we were swept up by the cloak of curiosity as we unrolled Vince's illicit stash and exhumed our solitary bud. I thumbed the stenchy button of weed into the hollow of another dented pop can and circled a lit match over it until it bloomed in a puff of smoke and fiery ember. I inhaled, coughed, hacked, spit, and inhaled again. Sherrod took his turn, and his own hacking fit seemed to betray his experience.

What happened afterwards is uncertain. I have no recollection of staggering from the smoky confines of the clubhouse, no recollection of wandering over the orange mound of the geyser, no memory of how we got from the clubhouse to the café, but we did. That much I do remember.

Outside, the day hunkered down as evening came our way and stars appeared in the skies. It was cold. Inside, the two of us ambled into the brightly lit café and sidled up to the lunch counter, eyes shot with blood, sick with laughter. Customers craned their necks our way, puzzled by our spectacle, and then resumed their conversations and toothpicks and coffee. And somehow, we managed to order cheeseburgers and Cokes, but it wasn't long— minutes, say—before my grandmother confronted us. "Look at me," she whispered. *"Look at me."* With my eyes half-clamped shut, I met her gaze. "What are you on?" She asked. Nothing, we assured her. Nothing. "Why are your eyes red?" Because the wind

97

was blowing. Because of the dust. "Finish eating and then get the hell out of here. You're lucky I don't say anything to your folks about this."

After an hour into *Gandhi*, Sherrod got up and left. I presumed that he had gone for popcorn or candy or a Polish sausage, but he never came back. Only when the three hour movie drew to a close, and the lights came on, did I realize that Sherrod had gone missing. I stumbled out of the theater dazed, sleepy, and somewhat confused. But when I pushed through the doors I saw Sherrod out on the sidewalk, shivering. "Where did you go?"

"I got kicked out."

"You got *kicked out*?"

"You don't remember?"

"No."

"I was barking like a dog!" He was amused at his own antics.

"*What*?"

"I was pretending that I was a dog. You don't remember?"

I was baffled. I had no idea. "Why'd you do *that*?"

"I don't know, man. But they kicked me out."

A shiver shot through my spine and rubbed my arms. "Have you been out here the whole time?"

"Until I started freezing my ass off, then I snuck into the lobby and hid upstairs in your hotel. But I didn't think the movie would be that long."

"You were in the hotel?"

"Yeah! What was I *supposed* to do? I couldn't go home. And I thought you knew I was kicked out and that you would come out, too."

"Did anyone see you?"

"Some old dude. Not your grandpa."

"That's good."

"I can't believe you didn't notice I was gone."

"I can't believe you were barking like a dog."

We laughed and crossed the street to the hotel. That night my grandmother said nothing and we said nothing. Sherrod took the hide-a-bed and I lay in my own. We whispered at length about girls, ranking them on scales from one to ten, and eventually drifted off to sleep under the skylight and the hum and breath of the building.

16. The Trapper

Soon winter was upon us and as a result I did fewer things, saw fewer movies, ventured out less and less. The air grew sharp and cold. The temperature plummeted to twenty degrees below zero while ground blizzards barreled through the streets. Local schools and a few businesses shut their doors. But the Enders remained opened. Inside the café and the lobby and the dining room, and throughout the entire building, heavy brass radiators banged and clanked as the furnace worked overtime to shoulder its heat through the building's maze of pipes. While the usual throng of regulars crowded into the café for coffee and omelets and breakfast steaks, my grandfather lay in his bed, completely reliant upon the oxygen that blew through the greenish-clear tubes running into his nose. The arctic temperatures showed no sign of letting up, and neither did my grandfather's emphysema.

But as the cold snap wore on, and as the heating bills soared, business slowed down proportionately. Fewer people wanted to wander out into the cold. Fewer people had the money to eat out. Layoffs seemed like an epidemic. Farmers were losing everything—equipment, land, homes. First Bank and Trust, the bank across the street from the Enders, the one we had banked with for three generations, and the one so many people had come to rely on, announced one day that it was going out of business. A large, national bank would take its place. Small mining plants shut down. Construction stalled. Kids in my school moved away. Even the bars that generally fared well during downturns faced their own problems as tabs went unpaid for months, and others were never paid at all. That winter, just before the cold snap, I was told for the first time in my life not to expect much of anything for Christmas.

Winter demanded constant work. The café opened at six o'clock in the morning, but my mother or grandmother would unlock the door at five thirty for the ranchers, farmers, and miners who wanted coffee before they set out for the day. In the winter it was my job to keep the sidewalks (front and back) and rear parking lot cleared of snow before our doors were opened for business.

Many mornings I was up at four thirty pulling on long johns, jeans, wool socks, boots, and gloves. Clothed and half asleep, I clomped outside to our gray cinderblock garage that squatted in the parking lot. I hunkered against the blowing snow and darkness, clutching a handheld propane torch and igniter. At the garage door, I turned the fuel knob slightly so I could hear it hiss, and squeezed the igniter until I saw the flame pop to life. And there in the blue glow of the torch, I warmed the padlock on the garage door, so I could wiggle in the small key and turn the lock's tumblers. Then, once I broke the padlock loose from the door clasp, I had to warm the latch-tongue and the clasp itself, and the doorknob, too. In the garage, I passed the torch flame over the graphite-gray auger on the snow blower to free it from the seize of winter. Everything was frozen.

I hated winter. Ours wasn't a family who saw winter for its recreational offerings: weekend ski trips, back-country fun, hot chocolate, hearthstones, brandy, or hundred-dollar sweaters. My family saw winter as something inescapable, a trap. Winter was a dangerous, ominous thing.

One morning, I fired up the snow blower—a large white and red machine with caterpillar tracks and three forward gears—backed it out of the garage, and drove it around to the front of the hotel. While the motor hummed, I gazed down the street at the traffic lights in the intersection. A snow plow blew by in a whorl of snow, scraping and banging along the empty, snow-packed roads. I turned and peered in the opposite direction, northward, up the street, toward the railroad tracks. The wind stung and numbed my face. I could see the dirty snow that had drifted over the black rails in patches, banks, and peaks. The street lamp above me wagged in the sudden gusts. I stomped my feet against the frozen ground to get the blood moving, clenched my teeth, and warmed myself on the hate I felt shoot through me. Just then I heard a whoosh and the unmistakable swashing sound of the geyser erupting. I walked to the corner of the building and looked down the alley toward the white, eighty-foot column of water enshrouded in a volcanic cloud of steam against the black sky. It was five o'clock. I skulked back to the idling machine, cranked the auger's spout streetward, and starting blowing snow.

Once the work was finished, I stowed the snow blower, shovels, and brooms I used for the doorways, shucked off my winter clothes, and headed inside for breakfast. Outside, the sun, still banked beyond Rabbit Hill, colored everything in gradient shades of crepuscule blue. In the café, I straddled a barstool at the counter among a row of men who were churning out a repertoire of banter, jokes, and gossip. At the time, while sitting on that barstool, I thought I was taking my spot in the world of men. My early morning grouchiness had waned. School was canceled as it often was in winter, and this felt good. It also felt good to be elbow-to-elbow in a place where the only thing that mattered was hard work.

That morning, there appeared a mangy old man at the end of the breakfast counter who wasn't a regular face among this group of locals. While I finished up my Polish sausage and eggs, I wondered who this guy was and where he had come from. He wore a ratty, sand-colored coat, and the clasps on his black rubber galoshes were broken and the toes were bound with duct tape. Fringed in ashen stubble, the old man's jowly face spilled around his mumbling mouth where his lower lip—oversized, purplish, and protruding—glistened with a line of drool. Two dark, deep-set eyes peered over his large, gourdish nose. His muttering, I noticed, grew louder, but no more decipherable, while he removed his greasy John Deere cap and scratched at his mat of gray hair. I noticed that he had ordered coffee but no breakfast. And even at the age of eleven I could surmise that this man probably couldn't afford breakfast had he wanted one, or worse, needed one. I guessed that he was probably homeless, and it was obvious, too, that he wasn't dressed for this kind of weather. He was just one in a string of men who seem to find themselves at the Enders, as if there were something beyond their control that drew them to this place. For a fleeting second I entertained the idea that this old man was my father. Flung at our feet, penniless. Belly-up in this gray world. Lost everything when he lost me. *This is what you get.* Our noses rubbed in the mess that has become his life. But I knew better. He didn't fit the picture I had stored in my mind. He was too old, too foolish. I looked at his boots again. He could die out there, I thought, as I cut through a piece of sausage with my fork. He really could.

I finished my breakfast and took a last drink from my hot chocolate. Janet, one of our morning-shift waitresses, came over and cleared my dishes. I liked Janet. Everyone did. She was older with auburn hair, green eyes, soft features, glasses, and always carried a smile and a quick joke. It couldn't have been easy, though. She and her husband, Ed, had lost one of their twin sons a few years before, when I was seven or eight. The boys—teenagers then—had been cleaning a hunting rifle when it discharged and killed the one boy, Charles. But to talk to Janet, or Ed, for that matter, you would never have known that such a tragedy had been laid at their feet, that such an irreparable loss had come their way. They were among the most pleasant people I had ever known, and she was one of the best waitresses we had ever hired.

"Can I get you anything else?" Janet asked.

"No thanks."

"Well," she said. "What are you going to do with yourself with no school today?"

"I don't know," I said.

"You don't know? Boy, I wish I had the day off. I could think of all kinds of things to do."

Out of the corner of my eye, I noticed the old man at the end of the counter get up and start to leave. He had left a mess of change, mostly pennies, on the counter for his coffee. "Thank you!" Janet called after him as he disappeared out the front door into the winter outside.

"I might get my sled out," I said.

"That sounds like fun."

Dad appeared in the lobby doorframe that connected to the café. I glanced at him and he summoned me with his finger. *Come here*, it said. He had donned his customary uniform: jeans and a belt from which hung a knife sheath (upside down so that with the help of gravity, the knife could easily slip out when the sheath was unsnapped), and a jangling set of keys, and a Dodge Ram hat clamped down over his jet-black hair—its bill impeccably tri-creased so that it looked like a walled tent. That he called me into the lobby meant I was in trouble and he didn't want to cause a scene in the café. I slid off the barstool and Janet tried to smile. The help was forever privy to the nuances of our family and our lives, and god only knows what they said about us—for better or worse—in our absence. I met my dad just inside the lobby. "Let's have another look at your work," he said. My stomach sunk. He had inspected my snow-clearing job and discovered that it did not satisfy his expectations. My work constantly failed to live up to his perpetually elevated standards, a fact that often sent him into violent rages.

I followed him, reluctantly, stupidly, through the lobby and through my grandparents' apartment and out the back door. In addition to clearing the sidewalks and parking lot, I also had to sweep out the doorways that led into the café, bar, apartments, the rear dining room door, and the café's basement doorway—all entrances that had screen doors, totaling nine in all. Should so much as a flake of snow remain in the doorway, it was my ass. If the snow accumulated, my dad reasoned (aided with a neatly penciled diagram illustrating the binding point), the storm doors wouldn't shut properly, and their hinges would spring and break. And that meant money.

He opened the dining room door and said, "Look."

I could see a dusting of snow against the kick-plate in the doorway.

"Did I ask you to do a half-assed job?"

"No."

"Then why is that all I get from you? Do I need to hold your hand, Brandon? Is that it? Maybe we need to hold hands until we learn how to work. Is that what you want?"

"No."

"Do you want to buy a new door?"

"No."

"Keep it up and that's what will happen. Because I'm not about to dole out for a new door because you're too goddamn lazy to do the job right. You got me?"

I looked at my boot and said nothing until he cuffed me across the side of my head.

"Look at me when I'm talking to you!"

I looked up.

"I said, *Do you got me?*"

I stared at him both terrified and defiant, holding my silence.

He cocked his arm back again and I cowered.

"Yes!"

"Yes, what?"

"I got you."

He stood there and stared at me with his yellowish eyes and finally said, "All right. When you're done, come get me, and I'll take another look. I want you to hit every door again and they had better be done right. And when you're done with those, don't go making any plans. I've got plenty for you to do today."

It took me nearly an hour to clean the rest of the doors out using a small whisk broom that I had found on some shelves in our back entryway. A regular broom's bristles were too coarse and too large to penetrate the narrow cracks in the wood and the ridges that lined the kick-plate. My lip began to quiver and everything looked bleary as tears rolled off my face and froze to the silvery plate, compounding the problem.

Later that afternoon I saw the shabby old man from the café. I was taking out the garbage when I spotted him rooting through the trash cans in the back parking lot. I slowed my approach and then heaved a bag into a large bin. Startled, he turned and stared at me, blinking quickly. "Oh," he said. "Hope you don't mind me snooping around here some. I was just looking for a bit or two for my traps."

"*Traps?*"

"For my trap line."

I swung the other bag of trash into the garbage can and said, "What do you trap?"

"Muskrat, mostly. Some beaver. Even a cougar now and again. That sort of thing."

"Huh," I said. "That's cool."

"Oh, it's something all right. A heap of work, too. But you can make good money if you know what you're doing," he said pointing to his head, emphasizing his last point about having the brains for the business. "It's certainly treated me fine for the last twenty years. You could say trapping is my life."

It did sound fun and exciting, and for whatever reason, the fact that he was a trapper justified, to my way of thinking, the way he dressed. Maybe he wasn't a bum or homeless. He was a trapper, a *real* trapper, another version of the Mountain Man that I had been learning about in Idaho History. My teacher, Mrs. Findlay, made it sound like mountain men and fur trappers were people from the past. Never did she mention or otherwise intimate that they still walked among us.

"You sell their furs?"

"That's right, boss. I sell their hides," he said as he put something in his coat pocket. I noticed that he mumbled between sentences as if he were rehearsing his lines.

"Where do you trap?" I could see him eyeing the trash can, the one I had just chucked the bags into.

"Pardon?"

"*Where* do you trap? Where do you get them?"

He mumbled while he looked off to the north toward S-Hill. "Oh, all around here. I got scads of traps. Good trapping in these parts. Plenty of varmints." He scratched the back of his neck and again looked off into the whitening distance. "Course, it's harder now, you know. With the market the way it is and all. Used to be a fella could get himself a good price on fewer hides. And now it takes more hides to get the same kind of pay-day. It's all economics, see."

I could see, and I couldn't see, so I just nodded and toed a small crust of snow at the edge of the black trash can.

"That's why I'm snooping here. Price of muskrat bait's gone out of sight, so I just as soon get what I can here—if it's all the same to you?"

I shrugged and said, "Sure."

He looked at the Enders, craning his neck back so he could see all the way to the top, and whistled. "Your folks run this *establishment*?"

I nodded. "Yeah. My grandparents own it, and my mom and dad help out."

"I bet you're swimming in the dough!"

107

"Not really."

"There," he said pointing to the back corner of the building and down the alley way. "Second one down. That's my apartment. Your granddad rented it to me."

He wasn't homeless after all, I thought. Not really, anyway.

He paused and thumbed his chin. "Let me see. You're, what, thirteen, fourteen, somewhere in theres, am I right?"

"Ten." The trash smelled sour and I tried to take in short, thin breaths.

"No kidding? I figured you older than that on account of your— maturity—and all."

"Nope. Just ten." I was getting uncomfortable and cold, and I wanted to go, but I didn't want to be rude.

He whistled again. "Listen, boss. Tell me your name."

"Brandon."

"Well, Brandon, I'm Jim. But you can call me Trapper Jim. That's what everyone calls me."

"Okay," I said.

He paused and looked around and clucked his tongue. "Say, I don't suppose you could help me out some?"

"With what?"

"I haven't had much luck finding anything in the trash that's— suitable—for my traps. Anything that's got any *substance*, you know." He pinched his grubby thumb and index finger together and rubbed some invisible substance. "I don't reckon you could help out along those lines?"

"Uh," I paused not knowing what to say, and not knowing what he really wanted.

"I'll make you a deal," he said quickly. "Let's say if you can get me some scraps, leftovers, that kind of thing, I just might be able to part with some of my traps, and you could go into business for yourself."

My own traps? I was elated. "Sure," I said. "I can get you stuff from the café, if you want, if that will work?"

"That'll work just dandy, boss."

In the back of the kitchen, beneath the industrial-sized stainless steel sinks, we kept a cluster of buckets and a gallon tin can. When the dishes came back from the tables in gray bus tubs, Betty, our dishwasher, scraped the food from the plates into the slop buckets and tossed any steak bones into the gallon tin for our dog, Ribbons. Once a week Bill Hines, a short, wiry man in his fifties who wore horn-rimmed bifocals and dark hair, hobbled into the café and hobbled out carrying the five-gallon slop buckets for his pigs. When business was good, Bill could count on five, sometimes six buckets of slop for the week. As a result, his pigs ate very well. But when business was slow, like it was that winter, he could count on two skimpy buckets, and sometimes only one. The same was true for our dog. When business was on the boom, people ate steaks, and Ribbons got steak bones at the end of the night. But when it was down, the tin can saw very few steak bones, and often none at all.

I could pinch Bill's slop buckets without anyone saying anything. My family, I knew, would frown on me consorting with Trapper Jim. So, if questioned, I could say that the scraps were for the alley cats that prowled around the Enders.

A couple of days after I first met Trapper Jim I saw him again at the trash cans. I was riding my sled off the low end of Geyser Hill into our parking lot, and a ground blizzard had just picked up. It was late afternoon and the sun had diminished to a pale disk in the gray. I had been outside for some time testing out my sled—a classic with red, steel runners, and wooden slats glossy with varnish. My gloves were wet and my nose was running, both signs that it was time to go in. That is when I heard a "Hull-*o*!" coming from the trash cans across the lot, and saw Jim waving his hands in case I didn't hear him over the howl of the wind. I stood, waved back, and grabbed the nylon rope tied to my sled's steering bar, and tramped over to Jim, my sled gliding behind me. Our dog, Ribbons, who had tired of our snow games an hour earlier opted to go back in where it was warm, otherwise she would have been barking at Jim, giving him the business.

"That's some outfit you got there," he said pointing to my sled.

"Thanks." I tamped my feet against the snow-packed lot. Snow blew around my legs and I felt a shiver run through me. "I got some stuff for you," I said. "I'll go get it."

"Sure thing, boss."

I trudged toward the hotel dragging my sled behind me and parked it on its end, against the orange brick of the building, just outside our apartment doorway. I walked three doors down and went into the café basement doorway and took the wooden stairs down into the warm, expansive—but dimly lit—storeroom. I took a deep breath. I could smell the earthen burlap and potatoes stacked in one-hundred pound bags on a pallet at the far end of the basement. Still their scent was new and fresh as if the potatoes had just been pulled from the earth, loam knocked from their skins. I had filled a gallon tin with scraps from Bill's buckets and stowed it under some supply shelves the day before. I snatched the tin, and took it outside to see if it met Jim's approval.

"I don't know what muskrat or beaver eat," I said. "But I tried to get the best stuff I could."

He jabbed his finger at the tin's contents—hunks of hamburger patty, chicken bone, bacon fat, bits of egg, baked potato, green beans—and smiled. "Top notch," he said.

I nodded and felt some relief. And then Jim did something totally unexpected. He snatched out a triangle of wheat toast and ate it. I looked at him dumbfounded, and he looked at me. "No sense in letting the varmints get at all of this," he said and winked.

He crouched and set the can in the snow, carefully, so it wouldn't tip, stood and rubbed his hands together for heat. "Now," he said. "Your traps." The trash cans stood in a row in front of a hedge of yellow rose bushes that divided our parking lot from the Senior Citizens' Center parking lot next door. Between the rose bushes and the garbage cans, Jim had stashed three traps, which he fished out for me. "And there you have it. You're in business now, boss," he said dangling the jaw-traps by lengths of chain before me. "That's as many as I can part with, but it's enough to get you started."

"Cool," I said reaching for the rust-colored steel traps.

"I figure a few more tins like this one and we'll be square."

I looked at him and nodded. That seemed right.

That same winter my aunt LaNae had fallen—again—on hard times, and so my grandparents put her and my cousin, Vince, in a tiny apartment next door to the bar, the one my parents had taken our first time back to the Enders. My aunt slept on a Murphy bed that folded down in the living room, and Vince slept on the couch two feet away from the foot of the bed. They had a stuffy bathroom and a tiny kitchen with a short, rounded refrigerator from the 1950s and a stove to match. LaNae was a great cook, so my mother and grandmother gave her a night shift in the café. She was a very likeable person with a terrific sense of humor, and a history of drinking. She also had a history of living with a string of abusive boyfriends with names like Igor and Ace. And after a few months or weeks of getting smacked around by these guys, she would pack up in the middle of the night and vanish. Somewhere along the line, LaNae would repeat the pattern and so on. Vince, at twelve, had already developed traits that mirrored, in some ways, his mother's. When he wasn't with his mother, he lived with his father until they had a disagreement, then he moved in with his grandparents on his father's side, taking a tiny bedroom in their trailer house outside of town on a bend of the Bear River. That arrangement would last until a blow-up occurred, and then it was on to another place with another relative. Over the years Vince had lived with us at least a half-dozen times. It would become a pattern that defined him.

At night LaNae cooked in the café, and then spent her wages in the bar next door to her apartment. Vince and I played together and hung out and got into trouble and then, inevitably, we would fight and not speak for days on end. One morning, for instance, I went over to their apartment while my aunt was out. Vince had the TV on and was cooking an egg on a battered and dented frying pan on one of the stove's coil burners. The dent in the pan was dramatic and caused the egg to run to one end where it broke. "Nice pan, man," I said.

He laughed. "Shut up. It still works."

"It's retarded," I said. "Look at your egg!"

"What about it?"

"It's totally screwed."

"No it's not. It's just fine."

"Vince, your pan sucks."

"So it's a little dented. Who cares? Besides, it's the only one we got."

"So get a new one."

"Why should we when this one works?"

"But it *doesn't*."

"Not everything has to be perfect, Brandon."

"I never said it did."

"Same as."

"Whatever." I walked out of the apartment and slammed the door.

Just like that something deep had boiled up to the surface and caused a silence that came from a place neither one of us could recognize. The argument was fast and flippant, the way of kids too close. If I felt shame I also felt assured, somehow, like I was standing in the tall sweetgrass on the better bank of a river that coursed through our family.

One night while at dinner in the café, the five of us sat at our usual table in the dining room—my grandparents, mother, dad, and I. The dining room was dark with rust and brown colored carpet and lavish red wallpaper with gold gilt and faux velvet bouquets. Antique lamps, brassy and dull in their light, yellowed the room.

Years ago, this is where Charlie was shot and killed, not seven feet from our dinner table. But that was then. When the dining room was the bar. When mother was serving drinks. When my own father was in prison. When Bud was drag racing other roughnecks through town. And when my grandparents were trying to reach their own respective shores of sobriety. That was then.

LaNae was cooking that night and when she put our orders up in the window, my grandmother put her menthol cigarette in an ashtray and said, "LaNae, damn it, take a break and come eat with us." Business was slow so it was a good time.

"Oh, thanks anyway, Mom. I already ate," she called back through the window. She dinged the bell.

"Where's Vince?" My mother asked no one in particular. "He's with his *father*," my grandmother whispered and lit her cigarette. She did not like Vince's father, and more than insinuated that he was to blame for all of LaNae's problems. Everyone else (with the exception of LaNae) liked him—a quiet, hard-working Polynesian man who liked to golf on the weekends. I thought he was cool because he drove a restored '56 Chevy, looked like Sylvester Stallone, and had webbed feet. He was muscular and wore shorts and tank tops and a soft smile. I thought he was unendingly cool but said very little in his presence. If I spoke it was usually to ask to see his webbed feet. "If your dad has webbed feet, why don't you?" I asked Vince once.

"I just don't."

"But your dad *does*," I insisted.

"And?"

"And why don't you?"

He laughed and called me a Clue, his standard shorthand for fool. When he didn't call me Clue, he usually called me Son.

After the waitress brought our food, I turned to my grandfather and said, "Did you ever trap when you were a kid?"

"Did I ever *trap*?"

"Yeah. Like muskrat or beaver or . . . cougar, anything like that?"

"No. Can't say that I did." He poured vinegar over a bowl of boiled spinach which was buttered and togged with black pepper and salt.

"We're learning about the trappers in Idaho History and I just wondered. What about you, Dad?"

"Eat your dinner," my mother interjected.

"No. Never had a need to," Dad said. "I guess I always thought it was kind of cruel, if you didn't have to."

"Trapper Jim says there's good money in it if you know what you're doing."

"Who?" my mother asked, her gaze shooting my direction.

"Trapper Jim. He's this trapper guy I met."

"Good god," my grandmother said. "That stinking puke?"

"*Who*?" Mother demanded.

"Jimmy Woodall. You know him. He's staying in Number 3."

My grandfather chuckled but said nothing.

"And what is so goddamn funny?" my grandmother asked him.

"He's okay."

"*Okay*? I don't have a sense of smell, and he makes me want to gag. And you haul off and rent him an apartment."

My grandfather shrugged and took a bite of his spinach.

"Oh, Jesus, Brandon. Stay the hell away from him. You'll catch a disease."

"He's nice," I said.

"He's a bum," my grandmother said, buttering a crescent roll.

"If he's a bum then why did he give me some of his traps?"

"What do you mean *gave you*?" my grandfather asked. His short gray hair was combed neatly back and his olive skin shone in the yellow light of the room. He wore slacks and a button-up woolen shirt.

"Excuse me?" my mother said. "And just what do you plan on doing with traps?"

"Trapper Jim said I could go into business for myself."

"Oh, no you're not," she said and wiped her mouth with a napkin.

"She's right, pard," my dad said. "I don't think it's such a good idea."

"Why not?"

"Because it is cruel and you don't have a need," he said. "Did old Jimmy tell you how animals try to get out of those traps?"

"No."

"They chew their own leg off. Imagine that for a minute."

"Let's not," my mother said.

For a half hour I appealed to them for a chance. I saddled myself with extra chores as an offering. I said that I could write a paper about it for my Idaho History homework—a school project. I could see, shockingly, that they were giving in. My grandfather was the one who suggested they let me try it for two weeks. A trial plan was set forth and agreed upon. I could set the traps before dinner every night, but I had to be up at four o'clock to check them so that not a single animal would be in jeopardy of suffering any longer than was necessary. The other stipulation: stay away from Jim.

By the time the cold snap let up, I had been trapping, officially, for four days. I strung my three beat-up traps along the tangled banks of Soda Creek. Trapper Jim had shown me how to work the traps—how to stand on the spring that opened the jaws, how to set the round trigger-plate, how to stake the chain into the creek bank where the edge hadn't frozen over. But that is where the tutelage ended. He didn't teach me what to do with a muskrat or beaver should the steel jaws of my traps catch one. He didn't teach me how to dress an animal, for instance, or how to treat the hides. This is what I thought about that first morning as I pushed through deep snow in the darkness, as I threw the weak beam of my flashlight on drifts and banks and other landforms that appeared strange and alien: snow-encrusted willow stands, dark junipers that looked hunched like bears, sagging fence lines fingered with ice.

With my dog, Ribbons, plowing behind me and yipping at an early thrush of northern shrikes, I felt my stomach rise and sink on undulations of anticipation and fear. I yearned to catch *something*, and was horrified by the thought that I actually would. I also wanted to impress my family, to distinguish myself as reliant, smart, and as a man. But my fear ran in both directions: If my traps were empty and I caught nothing, I would fail because I didn't know what I was doing. But if I dragged a trapped, snarling muskrat from the icy waters of Soda Creek, I would fail because I didn't know what to do with something like that. On the one hand I was inept, on the other, I was just cruel.

There was something else, though, despite all of this. As my eyes adjusted to the dark blue and to the stars that glimmered over this open and frozen sagebrush country, I couldn't help but feel satisfied that I was out here with the winter and not against it. I felt safer, somehow, among the brush and juniper and drifting snow than I did in the Enders where I dreaded the jangle of keys, the derision, the impossible expectations. Winter, I noticed, smelled different, cleaner, when I met it on my own terms. I loved the gnarled fields that swept out from behind the hotel. I made song out of the crunch of my footfalls over the snowfields. I took a comfort in the cadence and rhythms of this land away from the sour smells of my grandfather's bedroom; away from my dad's yellowish eyes; and away from the hollowness of that brick citadel that held us fast in its clutch.

When I approached the slushy creek bank and spotted the previous day's faint tracks that led to my first trap, I paused, breathed deeply, and trained my flashlight on Ribbons. Her long red hair was covered with snowballs. Steam rose out of her black nose and my light caught her brown expectant eyes. "Ready girl?" I said. She wagged her tail.

When I pulled the trap from the black water, I knew right away that the only thing it had caught were the frigid waters that flowed through its jaws. The same was true for the other traps. Nothing.

I felt humiliated. I *didn't* know what I was doing. I didn't even use bait—scraps from the Enders or otherwise. I just figured chance and chance alone would bring a muskrat into the design of these jaws, just as chance would surely bring my father to the Enders Hotel.

As it turned out, chance and my ignorance, kept them apart.

One morning on my way back from my trap line, I spotted Vince making a snow cave by the clubhouse. I got a late start that morning and it was fully light by the time I got back. Ribbons led the way while I dragged my sled behind, my three traps lashed to its slats. It must have been eight o'clock. I hadn't spoken with Vince since I stormed out of his apartment.

"Hey!" I called.

Vince poked his head out of the cave. "Check it out," he said. "We can nail anyone who walks by!" He was talking about snow-balling people from the snow fort.

"Cool!" I trudged over to the cave and started to help. In that strange fashion of boys, we said nothing of the thing that caused the days of quiet. There was nothing to say. And so we worked on the snow cave.

"What are those?" he asked, pointing to the sled.

"Traps," I said proudly.

"Like real ones?"

"This old guy—Trapper Jim—gave them to me."

"That guy's a bum."

"That's what Grandma said."

Ribbons barked and tore off after bird and sunk in a deep spot, high-centered.

"You know that shack behind my dad's house, the one that has the hoses and the lawnmower in it?" Vince asked, packing a snow-ball.

"Yeah."

"He used to live there."

"In the shack?"

"He didn't have no place to go, so my dad said he could sleep in there. He's a *bum*."

"Now he's in Number 3."

"Yeah, well, he's still a bum."

That morning was bright and cold with blue skies. I nodded and looked into the sky. The geyser bubbled and frothed on the hill behind us and stacks of steam lifted off the orange mound. The air smacked of sulfur as it always did because of the geyser, but the scent seemed subdued in the chill of winter.

"You catch anything yet?" Vince asked.

"Nah. I just like going out."

"Soda Creek?"

"Yeah. Lower."

Vince nodded. He knew the lower bends of the creek, and the meadows and pasturelands through which the stream meandered—choked with snow in the winter. He crawled out of the cave and beat his hands together. "Can I come?"

"How about this afternoon? I'm going out to reset these. Got to figure out some bait." My voice trailed off as I looked down and kicked at some snow.

"Cool."

That afternoon, I found myself in the café where it was warm. I had ordered some hot apple cider which I liked because it came in a small, ceramic teapot and that made me feel older, somehow. The café was quiet with only one or two customers. The brass radiators that stood beneath the picture windows started to clank and bang as the furnace kicked in. No one paid attention to these noises, to their song, and I did only vaguely. The only time people paid any attention to the radiators or the heating pipes is when my grandmother issued a wake-up call. Any guest who wanted a wake-up call was in for a real treat at the Enders, for the rooms had no phones and no clocks. Those guests desiring such an amenity were checked into the rooms directly above the café so when their hour came around, my grandmother would fish under the counter for a hammer and bang on the heat pipes that ran straight up through their rooms. Sometimes the customers were given a turn to whack on the pipes. This was good fun at our guests' expense. But that was the only time people noticed the radiators or the pipes that rose out of them. But on the quiet days, the slow and cold days, people just reached for their coffee or stared blankly out on to the snow-packed streets.

I had nearly finished my hot cider when the door opened and Frankie came in. He was two years ahead of me in school and his mom, Rose, was one of our head cooks. Frankie and I had become good friends. He was large for his age, had an infectious laugh, and wore glasses. His older brothers had both earned reputations as star athletes, and it was now left to Frankie to carry on those community expectations, which he did but to a lesser degree. When I first met Frankie he was waiting for his mom to get off a late shift. The high school football team—for which Frankie's brother was quarterback—was playing an away game and my grandmother told Frankie and I to go over to the apartment and listen to the game on the radio. When we walked into the apartment, Frankie said, "Do you really want to listen to the game?"

"No."

"Me either. Let's do something else."

So we spent the night creating impromptu skits and sketch comedy that we recorded into my old tape player. Each of us played a whole cast of characters and performed our own sound effects. We laughed all night long—playing and replaying our favorite scenes. At the end of the night, my grandmother and Rose were both puzzled that we hadn't listened to the game, but happy that we had got along so well.

Frankie straddled a stool just as I drained the rest of my cider. "What's going on?" he asked.

"Vince and I are going out to set my traps, out at Soda Creek. Wanna come?"

"What kind of traps?"

119

"Muskrat."

"Cool. Let me ask my mom." He stepped back into the kitchen and returned with a thumbs up.

Within an hour Vince, Frankie, Ribbons, and I were tromping over the snowfields toward Soda Creek. It would be dark in a couple of hours so we would have plenty of time. I remember that it felt good to have company along, others who were interested in what I was doing. Validation. I wanted to go a little farther west, to bends I hadn't yet trapped. The air smelled clean once we got away from the sulfurous breath of the geyser, and the sky was still clear of clouds. We scampered up the embankment to the railroad tracks, that great backbone, and my sled scraped across the ties and over the rails. Vince was the first one down the other side and Frankie pelted him with a snowball. Even though the cold snap had lifted, the temperatures held at their winter usual: eight to fifteen degrees below zero. A slight gust lifted my hair, and I stared down the railroad tracks. First to the west. Then to the east and a chill shot through me.

In all we crossed four barbed wire fences and one irrigation dam to get to the place where I imagined swimming muskrats. Some of the lower reaches of Soda Creek had iced over entirely, where the water pooled black under the shadows of willow. When we reached those places where it was most quiet, I stopped and said, "Here. I think this is good."

I felt giddy and confident. Vince and Frankie were just glad, I suppose, to be outside, away from the adult world.

"What do you use for bait?" Vince asked.

"Hamburger grease," I said looking over my shoulder. "I think that's what Trapper Jim has been using—more or less."

"Muskrats eat hamburgers?" Frankie asked. He and Vince laughed.

"No," Vince said. "I think they like sloppy joes."

I tuned them out as I trained my eye on a shadowy spot on the other side of the stream, a spot at the foot of an embankment. To get there, though, meant that I had to cross over a frozen spot, or walk a quarter mile back to the irrigation dam. I could cross. There had to be a place. I just knew it. While Vince and Frankie made jokes about muskrat diets and lobbed snowballs into the swift reaches of the creek where it hadn't frozen, I walked along the bank looking for ice thick enough to hold us. "We have to cross!" I yelled cupping my hand around my mouth.

"Are you nuts?" Frankie called back.

"Fuck that!" Vince yelled. "*You* cross."

I shrugged and continued my search. I knew I was lighter than either of them. After all, they didn't have to cross if they didn't want to. I turned back and noticed that they were following. I overheard Frankie say, "We better catch up to Skippy before he kills himself."

Finally I found a place that looked solid and secure enough to hold my weight. I tested the ice at the edge of the creek with my boot. Toe first. Then I knocked my heel against it. "See?" I said. "Solid."

"Yeah, right." Frankie said.

I felt confident because the ice did feel solid, so I stood on it and allowed my weight to settle. It was okay. But I was still at the edge. Slowly I scooted out toward the middle. At its widest, Soda Creek was only ten feet wide. This section was half that width. In the summer I could have jumped it. But in the winter, it might as well have been thirty feet wide. As I slid closer and closer toward the center, I felt more and more relieved. "Told you," I said out loud. That is when I decided to stomp. Once. Twice—.

When I broke through, my heart stopped. Everything stopped. My hands shot up and out. My feet hit bottom. I couldn't breathe. The black water was only chest deep, and there was no pull, no current to speak of. I remember Frankie and Vince on their knees in the snow at the creek's edge. I remember their mouths moving but the words were lost. Their hands rushed for mine. Mine reached back. Ribbons was barking. Everything seemed cast in the singular shades of a dream.

So this is how kids die, I thought.

Frankie and Vince managed to pull me out. I was beached in snow. My legs burned against the frozen denim of my Levi's. I wouldn't move for fear that my icy jeans would skin my legs down to the bone and shiny white joints. Frankie picked me up and said, "Come on. We gotta go." I couldn't walk on my own. That much must have been clear. I tried to talk but the words broke apart into an involuntary machine-gun chatter: *t-t-t-t-t-t-b-b-b-b-k-k-k*. My entire body started to shake and convulse violently. The only word I could finally utter with any coherence was "*C-c-c-c-c-o-l-l-d-d. C-c-o-l-l-d-d.*"

Both Vince and Frankie hauled me up the embankment to the railroad tracks. I remember some laughing. And I think Vince called me a "dumb-ass"—a lighthearted and well deserved scolding. And some encouraging words: "You're all right. Yeah. You're fine." I remember the Enders swinging into view. It seemed impossibly far away. And then I'm home. Just like that. In the apartment. On my back on the warm, green shag carpet. My legs burning. My mother is there. And Dad. I try to unbutton my frozen jeans but my red hand is shaking so uncontrollably that it's useless. I cannot even work it. It is someone else's hand. Someone in seizure.

My fruitless exploits in trapping ended soon after I fell through the ice, and still, the winter raged on. I pulled my rusty traps from a bank of snow outside of our apartment, knocked the ice off them, and retired them to the basement. I saw Trapper Jim less and less after that. And soon I learned that he checked out of Number 3, unable to pay his rent. The apartment had to be fumigated as he had dressed out animals in the kitchen, draped their hides over the edge of the bathtub, pitched their guts into the living room trash. At one point he had apparently asked my grandfather if he could use the café's kitchen to treat some of his hides and to cook up some of his game. And for a moment, my grandfather actually considered it until the wrath of my grandmother settled upon him. "I will shut down the entire building if you let him step one foot into my kitchen!" And that was that.

But on a bright Saturday afternoon, shortly after he checked out, I noticed something unusual and it made me think of Trapper Jim all over again. Icicles were crashing to the ground, and water trickled in the streets. The cold, it seemed, was lifting. It was a good day for sledding so I pulled on my long johns, boots, hat, and gloves. I summoned Ribbons and Vince and we headed outside into the sharp sunlight.

"Where's your sled?" Vince asked.

Steam rose from Ribbons's black snout as she surveyed the parking lot.

I had parked the sled against the brick building just outside our apartment window, and now it was gone. I looked around, confused at first, then panicked.

"Look," Vince said. He pointed to the snow. "Tracks."

A set of man-sized tracks led to the spot where the sled had been, turned around, and then disappeared down the alley at the side of the building, past Number 3. It was one thing to have another kid take something from you. I could have recognized that kind of trespass. That would have made sense. But to have an adult steal from you was a different kind of thing. I felt a lump fill my throat. I wanted my sled back. I knew who had taken it. There was no question about that. And I was angry and alarmed, betrayed even, and eventually saddened. He vanished of course. They all do. Left the Enders and trailed off into some horizon beyond that place.

17. The Ex-Con and the Ex-Professor

And so it followed that when one man left the Enders Hotel, another would take his place. I remember one in particular. His name was Vic. Like Trapper Jim, he seemed to have arrived as from the air itself. He was a large and lumbering man who wore a shock of charcoal hair, oiled and combed straight back. A chain smoker and heavy drinker, Vic was one in a long list of people who worked odd jobs for us. Decades before he checked into the Enders, Vic killed a man and served a lengthy prison term. Once paroled, he needed some stability, a foundation. We offered that for him. Most people would have turned him away. But Vic would never have gone to most people. He came to us.

I learned Vic's story the same way I learned the stories of many of our guests—in fragments. Neither my parents or grandparents ever sat down and told me someone's story in a complete narrative, start to finish. It was impolite to talk about anyone at that length. I suppose it felt less gossipy, less indulgent if they ladled out their story intermittently, in abbreviated turns. Generally, I took what I heard and filled in the holes with my own observations. The fragments of Vic's story filtered down to me this way:

He was in the pen. Killed someone. Intelligent. Has a teenage daughter. Has a temper. I took note of the tattoos that inked his forearms, the time he spent in the lobby phone booth talking, I presumed, I hoped, to his daughter. The far-flung father calling home. Then I tried to align this information with the stories and rumors I had heard about him. There were always stories. I watched him in the lobby or as he slipped into the bar. I spied on him through the keyhole in the French doors of our apartment.

My mother kept her guard around Vic, and my dad exchanged idle words with him. But despite the rumors, my grandparents liked Vic. Even when the help were terrified of him, skittish in his presence, their voices a quavering warble of forced politeness. Even when he pulled a knife in our bar one night, and my petite grandmother had to talk him out of opening the guy right there on her floor—even then, he kept in good favor with our family.

That summer between our fifth and sixth grade years, B.J. and I worked for my grandparents around the hotel making it inevitable that we would cross paths with guests, customers, maids, waitresses, cooks, bartenders, drunks, and drifters—people like Vic. Our jobs were as varied as they were demanding. Slopping hot tar on the pan-flat roof with long-handled mops, chipping gray paint from doorways and eves, hoisting buckets of lathe and plaster down from the third story fire escape. Raking two dump-truck loads of fresh red cinder across the expansive parking lot by hand. There was always something. But the rules of our work never wavered: Do your job. And don't bother anyone. At the end of the day, we appeared before my grandfather who would pull out his handmade leather wallet, pluck out two twenty-dollar bills, and send us on our way. Of course neither B.J. or I could spend that money fast enough, indulging ourselves in any luxury that exuded instant pleasure: strawberry milkshakes at the drugstore, candy, Cokes, and cigarettes we bought from the vending machine over at the Caribou Lodge.

One afternoon we had been at B.J.'s house fooling around with a slingshot he got at a swap meet. "Let's take it down to the club-house and hit some shit," he said. On our way to the fort, we saw a man sleeping on the grass in a park by the geyser. Geyser Park was not much of a park, really. It was more of a narrow strip of grass with a one-way street hooked around it in a perfect U. Situated at the southern edge of the hotel parking lot, the park offered a place for tourists to stop, picnic under weeping willows, and watch the geyser go off. The man lay directly beneath those trees. I knew who he was because my grandmother or grandfather told me who he was. B.J. and I stopped in a skid, and stared at him. "That's Wil-lie," I said. "He's a bum."

"Looks like a bum," B.J. said.

"Used to be professor down to ISU."

"Jesus."

"Yeah."

"What a fucking loser."

"No shit."

His glasses were cocked on his face, and thin shadows from the willow branches fingered across his forehead. Flies buzzed his nose and gray mustache and gray lips.

Soda Springs had (and has) a handful of people you might call town drunkards and Willie Carter was one of them. He was tall, had silverish-brown hair, and always looked gaunt. His face hung in grisaille shades of gray like it had been lifted from a fresco. He wore metal-rimmed glasses with brown lenses. He donned suit trousers, a button-up shirt, and red suspenders crisscrossed at the back.

"Watch this shit," B.J. said. He bent down, snatched up a chunk of red cinder, and buried it deep in the slingshot's leather thong. He stretched back the Wrist-Rocket's cords with his elbow fully cocked, and let it fly: *Whap!* We heard the chunk of cinder smack Willie in the ribs. "Holy shit!" I said, grinning.

Willie let out a moan and rolled over, seemingly unfazed. We took off on our bikes laughing so hard we could barely pedal.

It wasn't long before it turned into a game, a way to pass our afternoons. *Let's go fuck with Willie,* we'd say. The highest point on Geyser Hill is an old spring that died out, and looks like a six-inch deep volcanic crater with the diameter of a manhole cover. It is covered with patches of black lichen, and tiny springs bubble around its perimeter. Dubbed "Eagle's Nest," this favored lookout spot rises some thirty feet directly above Geyser Park. From there we could see almost everything—the back of the Enders building, the railroad tracks that cut through town, the phosphate mine to the north, a sea of rooftops, stands of cottonwoods and box elders, and of course, Geyser Park and its resident, Willie, who had made it a habit of passing out on the grass.

One day we socked a hundred or more bottle rockets, a lighter, and a longneck Coors bottle into a duffel bag and scurried from our clubhouse up to Eagle's Nest where we had a good aim at Willie. At thirty feet, he was an easy target. One after another we fired the rockets at Willie and watched them explode into a fit of smoke and shredded paper. We took turns shooting. Time and again, we nailed him. One in the crotch, and one in the ribs. One in the arm pit. One in the neck. Several to the legs. A gut shot. Each one seemed better than the last, each one exploding into confetti. Willie flailed drunkenly and kicked in the bright green grass under that summer sun. He shrieked and cursed and spat. We had never laughed so hard in all our lives. Our arsenal spent, we simply wiped a few tears from our eyes and said, "Now what?"

One day bled into another as that summer burned on. We shot water snakes with our pellet pistols, and dragged their tangled mass in gunny sacks a quarter-mile from the spongy banks of Soda Creek back to the clubhouse where we lopped off their heads. With our pocketknives, we split open their white bellies, scooped out their entrails, and pitched them into the June grass where they drew a blue veil of summer flies. We tacked the snake skins to warped wooden planks with rocks and crooked nails, and set them on the roof of the clubhouse to dry under the baking sun.

We wanted to make snakeskin belts or boots and sell them at the next swap meet, but in a matter of days, the skins brittled and blew away into a hot wind. On alternate days we squatted in the dank recess of our clubhouse, where we smoked Lucky Strikes, looked at *Playboys*, talked about junior high girls, or listened to Rock 103 on my battery-powered radio.

That was also the summer we began dumpster diving behind the bars. Counting ours there were three bars on our side of the block. And their trash cans contained the detritus of the secret adult world, clues that hinted at forbidden rites. You can learn a lot about adults by observing what they keep, but you can truly know them for what they discard. We fished out any number of telling remnants—toothpicks that looked like swords, lipstick tubes, cigarette lighters, busted pool sticks, playing cards boasting naked ladies, and on and on. But what we sought most of all was liquor. The bottles the bartenders tossed weren't completely empty. In fact, we learned that if we collected enough like-bottles and accumulated their residual contents, we would, over time, have enough to get drunk on. We gathered Jose Cuervo bottles, Popov Vodka, Jack Daniels, Southern Comfort, Crown Royal, and Black Velvet. Over the course of that summer we had several ounces in each. On weekends we mixed the booze in our Pepsis that I lifted from the café, got tipsy, smoked some cigarettes, and veered our bikes into the night looking for something to happen under that sky, so moon-slung and wild with stars.

Like so many men before him, Vic asked my grandfather time and again to help him stop drinking. One alcoholic to another. "You've got to want to, Vic," my grandfather had said. "That's the only way I know of." It was a common thing, the swaying figure rattling our door at two in the morning, begging for help, that sour stench of men, of piss and booze, spilling into our apartment. The darkness suddenly rich with the scent of brewing coffee. Cigarette smoke. Lulled conversations. Sometimes weeping. Once it's Vic.

Once it's my parents. Once it's B.J.'s dad. He was wrecked, he had said. Needed thousands of dollars to save his home. My grandfather gave him the money. Never got it back, never expected to. That was another unspoken world. Something I knew but never told B.J. Something he might have suspected but never said aloud. Still, my grandfather took these men in, talked to them, and drove some of them, the earnest ones, fifty miles to Pocatello in the frail light of morning where he would check them into treatment. He took with him on those drives a pot of coffee and two things he kept in our kitchen cupboard but never used: a pack of filterless Camels or "studs," as we called them, and a pint of Everclear. "Sometimes they need it. To get them there," he told me once. I remember putting that dusty pint to my lips one day and jerking when the ravenous liquor touched my tongue. Some of it splashed in my eye. It burned my skin and I never touched it again, preferring instead the stuff we pulled from the dumpsters and diluted with cola. I knew somehow that when a man like Vic put that pint to his lips, he wouldn't jerk like I did. I admired that and feared it, too.

One day during that summer, I crossed paths—literally—with Vic. I was in the lobby on my way into the café, and he was on his way into the bar. A powdery blue, short-sleeved, button-down shirt hung loose over his dark jeans. He fixed his eyes on me in an unflinching squint. I noted his nose, large and red, and how crow's feet raked out from his temples. A cigarette hung from the corner of his mouth. He eyed me up and down, and then chuckled. He reached out, palmed my head with his large hand, and mussed my stringy straw-colored hair. "Where's Granddad?" he asked. I was eleven years old and terrified of Vic because of his size and presence, and because of what I knew. "I dunno," I said. "Maybe in the apartment."

"You keeping your nose clean?" he asked and inhaled a drag.

"Yeah."

He nodded and his right eye clamped shut against the smoke while he forced his massive hand into his jeans pocket. He pulled out a green, rubbery coin purse and squeezed it open. He jabbed at its contents with his index finger, snatched out a fifty-cent piece, and flipped it to me. But I was too slow, fumbled, and dropped it. I crouched, grabbed the coin, and looked up at Vic who was jamming his purse back into his pocket.

"Don't spend it one place, huh?"

I nodded and said, "Thanks."

I do not know why Vic gave me that fifty-cent piece. But I felt both vaguely satisfied and alarmed. Satisfied that he had drawn me into his confidence and had given me something. Alarmed that he noticed me at all, that he touched me, that I had locked eyes with him, and that there was now something between us.

Later in the summer, B.J., his older brother, David, Sherrod, and I were kicking through Geyser Park en route to the clubhouse when, on a whim, Sherrod shimmied up the trunk of a weeping willow. We paid little attention until he jumped out of the tree and yelled, "Jesus, you guys! Check it out!" Sherrod held two brown paper sacks, each containing a pint of vodka. I knew what it was. It was Willie's stash. Finding that vodka was like finding a suitcase filled with hundred dollar bills. It was beyond our paltry collection of dumpster booze—so random and unexpected. It was a gift.

That afternoon all of us rode our bikes east of town to Ledge Creek. We stripped down to our white underwear, found a deep, cool spot in the creek, and jumped in. We thrashed around in the water, then got out, and mixed the vodka in paper cups with cola. We held guzzling contests and diving contests. Guzzle a cup, dive into the creek. Get out and repeat. I remember cannon-balling off of a culvert pipe that emptied into the stream. I plunged into the deep part of the pool where the water's surface looked as black as obsidian. It felt good with the water over my head. I could see the flickering, foreshortened images of B.J., David, and Sherrod standing on the edge of the rusted culvert pipe. I could hear them talking. But their words were muted and garbled like dialogue in a dream. I let myself sink to the bottom. Bright green scarves of moss

wavered in the glimmering pool and I could feel their tendrils lick-
ing my sharp, white ankle bones. Everything was cool and quiet
and clear and clean. Then B.J. jumped in. I dug my foot into the
pebbly bottom and shot to the surface, gasping.

"Dip-shit!" B.J. said. "Are you trying to drown yourself?" He
slapped his hand on the water splashing me in the face. We both
laughed and got out, scrambling up the muddy bank, and continued to drink. All of us drank until we were running naked through
the dark reed grass, stirring up indigo dragonflies and yellow-
headed blackbirds. Sunburned and covered with mud and scrapes
and cuts from bulrush, thistle, and rocks, we finished or mostly
finished the two pints. And there in the middle of rural Idaho we
stood naked in a circle, sick on Willie's vodka, with stupid, slackened smiles dangling from our faces like field sickles; and there, on
the weed-choked edge of the world, we pissed on each other, dous-
ing ourselves in hot streams of urine under a full, yellow sun.

I did not think about Willie Carter again until I saw his bloody
body in Geyser Park one morning on my way to school. Fall had
come and the morning was cool. Two police cars and an ambulance idled near the park. Their radios squawked. Willie had been
knifed several times in the middle of the night. Farmers in the café
would later say that he had been "rolled." I rode by slowly, watching the EMTs load Willie's bloodied, motionless body into the
ambulance. To me everything was quiet but a morning wind that
stung my eyes and wailed in my ears as I pedaled into it. It was so
cold and clean I thought I could drink it, thought I might drown
in it. Gray willow branches rattled and clicked above, and inside, I
felt my stomach sink.

Some say it was Vic who rolled Willie, that it was the thick-
chested ex-con who took a knife to the old man. It was Vic, the
man who rented a room upstairs, the one who had a daughter out
there somewhere. It was him. People knew it was Vic as surely as
they knew what season it was. He rolled him, they said. He took a
Buck Knife and sliced him up, they said. And for what? For money,

booze, or spite? Because Vic himself was restless or callous, or worse, indifferent? Because Willie mouthed-off to him? Made a comment? Because he had bothered him?

Willie survived and Vic disappeared. Vanished. It is like he had taken his knife—still brown with Willie's blood—slit open the white sky, stepped through, and closed it behind him. Maybe he thumbed his way across rural highways to find his teenaged daughter I had heard about. Or perhaps he found another crumbling hotel in another crumbling town, a place he could throw down a bedroll and ward off whatever it was that haunted him.

As autumn again turned into winter, and as temperatures dropped, I spent less time with B.J., and more time in the Enders by myself. On some nights I read books or magazines or hung out in the café. I flipped through my baseball cards. I did what boys do. But occasionally, when caught unaware, I found myself panicked by the possibility that Willie might come in the café and order some coffee, that he might see me. Some men I hoped to see one day in our lobby or at the yellow lunch counter, and others I feared I would see all too soon. Finally, the fear that felt most real, the one that swam in my stomach, was that any one of these broken men could be my father. The man who shot and killed his best friend in our bar, or his friend who died on our sidewalk. Or Willie or Vic or any of the others to come.

Willie was a weak and core-sick man, and I was a boy sick on the idea of manhood. It was all around me. But I could no more enter that world than I could steer my bike into the sky. No more than B.J.'s dad could save their house or Vic stop drinking. They are settled things. There are other settled things, too, like how boys behave. What I did to Willie was cruel but also a kind of rite, a way to touch the world of men, and have it touch back.

18. Legacy

One day my dad got off the phone with the Union Hall, looked at his notebook, and said, "Alaska." We would move there. The work was good, the money great, and the schools topnotch. "Just imagine," my mother said. And I did. I returned to my nautical map I had exhumed from the basement, and put my palm to its thick, water-stained paper. I traced imaginary paths through the unknown land, plotted adventures. My thoughts conjured images borrowed from the Jack London stories I had read. But ultimately, the dream dimmed. The last thing I wanted to do was pick up again and move that far away. I couldn't. I wouldn't, and I said so emphatically. Days later it was decided that my mother and I would stay, and that Dad would go off to the tundra, to a place with blue glaciers the color of bottle glass. It was a place of white nights, they said. Ours was a place whose nights were orange with slag-glow, and I was relieved and surprised that I would stay.

So it was on a quiet Sunday morning during my fifth grade year that Dad loaded his green Dodge pickup with his tent, backpack, a .22 ("for plinking"), sleeping bag, boots, camp shovels, and his chest of tools. Without ceremony we said our goodbyes and waved as he idled out of the Enders parking lot under the hush of gray morning sky. I stood there in a chill breeze and wondered if he would ever return.

My grandfather then became the one who would usher me into the ways of the world in Dad's stead. On his good days when he wasn't strapped to oxygen—those days becoming fewer by the number—my grandfather and I would drive out to the family ranch. Where the hot pavement ended and the gray tongue of gravel road began, we pulled over, time and again, and switched drivers. That is how and when I learned to drive a stick shift— either in his red Volkswagen Rabbit or small, yellow Ford pickup. It was imperative, he and my grandmother agreed, that I learn how to drive. Should he collapse, fall, stop breathing, anything, I would need to get him back. I would need that kind of knowledge. Day after day I drove the winding gravel road that carved through endless fields of barley. In the spring we would drive the narrow, slot canyon road, walled in by the flickering green light that the newly leafed aspens threw across the car's hood, and park in a grove. He liked to walk beneath that wash of green dappled light and stand at the edge of the canyon creek whose cold waters shone bright and winked like a ribbon of coins. Sometimes he gathered wild mushrooms. Sometimes he just stood there; feet in the grass, face in the wind.

Alternately, we would stop at the fish pond on the ranch, the one he built and stocked with trout, and I would skip rocks across its brightening surface while he made his way to the field's edge. I would watch him, my eyes asquint in the sun, as he crouched, and tested the loam with his fingers, silent in all that land as if he were channeling it and the generations that had brought it forth. And when I finished skipping rocks, I would scurry up a hill on the other side of the road, and kick my way through tufts of silvery lupine and rabbit bush to a thicket of wild gooseberries. I plucked the ripe green berries from the branches and popped their sugary tart bodies into my mouth while keeping one eye open for snakes.

Snatching up a handful of the fruit for my grandfather, I would skitter down the hill back to the car, and we would drive on looking out at the fields that swayed beneath a wind.

What I liked best about those drives were the stories he told, stories about his years on the ranch. He would sit in the passenger seat spitting brown tobacco juice into a Styrofoam cup while scanning the landscape, his chest heaving and fighting for more air. His stories had a cadence governed by his breath. He would issue two or three sentences and pause for two long breaths, and deliver three more lines, and in this way he told me many of his stories. Of growing up in this land before World War II. Of the whiskey still his father built in Sulphur Canyon. Stories of when he returned from Germany to the ranch and took over the sheep operation. And stories of lambing in the spring. All the while I kept my eyes on the road, my hands clamped around the steering wheel and my sneaker nuzzling the accelerator. A great plume of dust stretched out behind us as we drove deeper into that country.

One of my favorite places on the ranch was an enormous system of lambing sheds that squatted between one of the two ranch houses and the Quonset hut. I remember how they smelled like earth and dung and how burlap bags of wool crowded pens, and how sheets of sunlight fell through the roof slats exacting a geometry of shadows on the wooden floor planks. Very often I would get to spend a few days on the ranch with my Uncle Jerry and my cousins Jade and Angel. We would wile away entire afternoons in those sheds. Or we would picnic in one of the abandon sheep camp trailers that stood in a stand of aspens down the lane from the dooryard, and we would wade through the tallgrass to get to them. The trailers were compact and hot and flies buzzed the windows as we ate cold fried chicken or ham sandwiches and slices of watermelon and potato chips. From there we would hike to the junkyard where the remnants of the generations were discarded and overgrown in thistle and morning glory. Old combine harvesters rusted to the color of blood, flatbed trucks sitting on rotten tires, wooden balers with sunken spoked wheels, or a chance deer carcass—an undone puzzle of sun-bleached bones. Like the suitcase room in the Enders Hotel, that junkyard held the vestiges of all the untold stories—the ones of promise, and the darker ones, too, those of gun accidents and diphtheria and dead children. All of them whispered there in that ghost yard. It's little wonder that as children we felt its pull, that we ended up there day after day, the wind tugging at our hair.

And when we kicked rocks down the lane or struck sticks against old machinery, I felt the sting of envy shoot through my stomach when I looked up and saw my cousins standing atop an old grain truck—their small bodies just heavy enough to dent the rusted roof. At moments like that, I wanted to be them, to have their last name: Beus. Because this, all of this, the thousands of acres of barley, the corrals, the streams, the junkyard and Quonset, the orchard, ranch houses, bunkhouse, and meadows—all of it— was theirs. Or would be. It was the natural order of things. They looked like their father who looked like my grandfather, and his father, Albert, before them. Jade's middle name didn't come from the doctor who delivered him, but from his great-grandfather, Albert, and I envied that, too. They had the same Italian nose, a "wop nose," my grandfather called it, quickly adding, "Don't ever say that, though. It's not nice." Wop nose or not, I wanted it. When Jade—not Angel, on account of her sex—took over the Beus ranch, as he one day would, he would be the fifth generation of Beuses to work this land. My name—Schrand—had nothing whatever to do with any of it. This was not my place. And so I would console myself that the Enders Hotel was my place, and that it would one day be mine. That it was my legacy.

Sometimes my grandfather and I would drive north of town to Hooper Springs. We took a plastic jug and I would fill it with the cold roiling mineral water, cupping a handful of it to my mouth and flicking my hand dry into the dark green grass. One subject that often arose on those afternoon drives was the subject of water. "If you want to know who has power out here," he'd say, "don't look at their houses or the trucks they drive, look at their water rights. Out here, water is everything." He was rich in water rights. Still, his engineer's mind kept puzzling over his two pet projects. How to better irrigate his ranch, and how to heat the hotel by using steam from the geyser. Invariably, on those drives, he would draw me into his plans. "I'll give you a hundred dollars if you can design a gravity-feed system to irrigate the fields below the dooryard." The same offer stood for heating the Enders, though he knew that using mineral-rich sulfur water would not work. But this was beside the point. The point was to keep my mind working, although I saw the challenge as a way of including me in the business of the hotel and the ranch, which made me swell with pride.

When we returned from the drives, my grandfather would retire to his room, turn on the oxygen tank, and doze through the still hours before dusk, while I sat down with a sketchpad and a cup of crayons trying to imagine the world of water and gravity and how I might capture it on paper.

19. Two Men in a Car

One day my grandfather checked two men—traveling workers in town for spot labor—into the hotel. They had been seen in the café for dinners, milling in the lobby, working their teeth with toothpicks, or in the bar, but they never drew much attention to themselves otherwise.

I noticed them shortly after they arrived, and studied them. They were maybe in their late forties and looked hard. One wore a ratty mustache and the other was short and compact and balding. When they talked it was usually to one another, and they kept their voices to a low drone.

One morning my grandfather was up at his usual early hour when the sky was still dark but for a faint blue glow to the east. He poured some coffee and happened to look out into the hotel parking lot from his bedroom window. A rusted, white Pontiac sat idling, its windows steamed over. As the blue glow in the east moved west, he could make out two figures in the car's front seat. An hour passed. Then two. Then three. The figures had not moved and the car kept idling. Concerned, my grandfather slipped on his loafers and jacket and stepped outside into the chill of dawn.

His cold-knuckled raps at the glass did not elicit a response, so he knocked harder, and harder again. When he opened the door and stuck his head in it appeared at first glance that the men, the same two he had checked into the hotel, were fast asleep. But when he felt for a pulse under the driver's chin—the man with a mustache—there was none and his skin was cold. The same was true for the passenger.

They were both dead.

It all happened very quietly. A phone call to the police chief. A quiet investigation. And the answer: carbon monoxide. They had either passed out in the car or had fallen asleep but it was most certainly an accident, the chief said. And before the regular breakfast crowd streamed into the café, the rusted white Pontiac was emptied of its bodies, the rooms upstairs emptied of their personal effects, and the car was towed away as casually as it had arrived. No newspaper story. No lunch-counter gossip. Just a few leaves of paperwork, some carbon-copy, a signature, and that was that.

20. Substitute

I wanted my diagrams of the gravity-feed system to be as neat and ordered as the diagrams my dad kept in his notebooks—those that mapped electrical conduit in the hotel basement, that Byzantine network of unending, mysterious, impossible circuitry. Or those that tackled plumbing, or a leaking radiator in one of the cars. But mine did not compare. My diagrams were sloppy and foolish and childish. My lines weren't straight like Dad's, and weren't labeled with corresponding measurements and dimensions. My lines wandered and thickened when my crayons dulled. But the diagrams gave me something to talk about when Dad called home on Sunday evenings from Alaska. "I'm helping Grandpa with the gravity-feed system," I said. "He's gonna give me a hundred bucks if I can do it. If I can design it."

"All right, pard! That'll keep you out of trouble," he said and laughed.

Although I was embarrassed by my sketch, I presented it to my grandfather all the same. His bedroom door was closed but I could see that his lamp was on through the obscured windowpanes. When he looked at my drawing, he took great care. He pulled his eyeglasses from their sheath in his shirt pocket. He sat up. Each movement costing him more air. His face looked taut, swollen. My sketch rattled like an aspen leaf in his quaking hand. His chest rose and fell. "That's the idea," he said. "Now you just have to get the water in the sprinklers." He handed it back and removed his glasses. We sat on the edge of his bed and stared quietly across the expanse of parking lot espying the geyser's continual crashing froth and how it cascaded, one rippling sheet after another, into the drainage canal.

That was the summer, too, when my mother flew to Alaska to visit Dad. Her fear of flying was only matched by her fears of my being kidnapped, a great earthquake that would kill us all, or nuclear war with Russia. But she couldn't or wouldn't drive to Alaska, so that left flying. When she came home she had pictures. She and Dad standing in a wash of wild grass blazing with flowers like stars in the sky. Another shows the Mendenhall Glacier in the background. They look happy. "Oh, Brandon," she said of Alaska, "You would have just loved it. But it's good to be back. To be *on the ground*," she added laughingly, and stubbed out her cigarette.

My mother was happiest when she was busy, and so she courted every demand the Enders made of her time. Deep in the kitchen she had carved out a space for herself. And she carved out space for me too. During the school year I was to do my homework in the café where she was close by. After school I reported to the back of the kitchen to check in: How was school? Did I have any homework? What were my plans? These are your chores. If she was good at anything it was cooking and running a kitchen. She knew these skills as if they had been genetically encoded. And she loved the work and treated it as an art. Each lemon meringue pie, scone, Belgian waffle, or rack of homemade noodles an exhibit to be displayed. Aesthetics mattered. But substance mattered more. Work was the drug that filled the place alcohol had taken before. The same was true for my grandparents. The work was something to get lost in.

The Enders Hotel was something of a halfway house for many

people including my own family. AA meetings took place in the dining room, and half of those who attended had or would at some point stay in the hotel and work for my grandparents. One evening my grandmother called me into the dining room where she and a waitress were setting up the tables for a meeting. Several thermoses of coffee and pitchers of water were placed on the U-shaped tables. Silverware rolled in white napkins along with cups and water glasses marked each place setting. In the far corner of the dining room stood a stack of chairs. "Make sure each place setting has a chair," my grandmother said. So I moved chairs quickly, taking pride in my efficiency. Slowly, people started to arrive for the AA meeting and my grandfather came over from the apartment and introduced me around. Everyone made a big fuss about me and I blushed. They made the fuss because I was the grandson of Lynn and Beth Beus. "Jerry's boy?" they would often ask, meaning my uncle Jerry—and not my father by the same name.

"No," my grandmother corrected. "Karen's."

"*Ah*," they would say.

I was pleased anytime I was mistakenly assigned to the Beus family because it meant that to some people, I actually passed as a Beus.

Soon the dining room filled and one man who seemed to have taken charge, smiled at everyone, and said, "Well? Should we get started?"

I took this as my cue to leave. I understood the confidential nature of these meetings and intuited that they were not the place for kids. But when I turned to leave, my grandfather looked at me and said, "You can stay if you want."

All eyes were on me and my face filled with blood. "Really?"

"Don't see why not. You know the rules."

I did know the rules. What was said there, stayed there. First names only, et cetera. I hesitated and then the adults started goading me to stay. "Come on," they said. "We don't bite!"

So I took a chair next to my grandmother.

"We would like to welcome our new visitor," the man in charge said looking toward me. "Brandon is Lynn and Beth's grandson for those of you who just arrived." The man had sandy hair and glasses and dressed neatly. He was thin and warm and his smile seemed genuine, grateful even. I liked him immediately. He started to talk first and then everyone else took turns or passed (like my grandparents), and eventually it was my turn to speak. I stood and said my first name as everyone else had done and was received with a resounding, "Hi, Brandon." And I started to tell my story and what I had seen. "Maybe what I have to say doesn't matter as much because I'm just a kid, but I've grown up around alcoholics and I have seen what happens. Even just living here next to a bar and in a hotel. I see lots of stuff." I talked and made a couple of attempts at jokes and everyone laughed and when I sat down everyone clapped. Afterwards they all came up to me and thanked me for my story and the courage it took to say what I had said. "You must be proud," they said to my grandparents.

"We are *most* of the time. When he's not being a little *you-know-what*," my grandmother teased.

After everyone had gone, I helped my grandmother gather coffee cups and saucers and pie plates and glasses and cart them into the café in gray bus tubs. "I liked the man in charge," I had said to my grandfather. "He was really nice."

"He is a helluva guy. Really is. He stayed here for awhile when he was quitting. Did some work for us, too, until he broke his leg."

"How'd he do that?"

"Fell off the roof."

"He fell off the roof?"

"Yeah, lucky it didn't kill him."

"What was he doing on the roof?"

"Tarring."

I was stunned. Whenever I was on the roof, I would peer over the edge certain that no one could survive a fall from that height.

Not long after the AA meeting, my grandfather came in the café with an elderly man with clean skin and white hair and dressed very well. He was nice and quiet and shook my hand as if we had known each other a very long time and this was a reunion and not an introduction. But I did not recognize him at all. If I had seen him in the café or hotel for that matter, he didn't stick out like the others did, like the roughnecks, those who, to my thinking, matched the profile of my father. My grandfather told me his name, and I said it was nice to meet him.

"He'd like to take you fishing," my grandfather said.

The man looked at me expectantly, and I looked back at him and then at my grandfather. I could see that I didn't have a choice in the matter.

"Uh, yeah. Sure. When?"

"How about this afternoon?"

I looked out the large café windows and the day was filled with sunlight. "Okay."

My grandfather and the man disappeared into the lobby, and I slipped into the kitchen and walked past Rose, the cook, and Betty, the dishwasher until I reached the back end of the long narrow kitchen where my grandmother was chopping celery.

"When are you going?" she asked, referring to the fishing trip.

"This afternoon."

"Good."

"But—who *is* he?"

"He's a friend your grandpa helped a long time ago. Got him into AA."

"Oh."

"It will be good for the both of you."

"It's just—weird. You know."

She stopped chopping and wiped her hands on a white towel. "When he was drinking he lost everything. His job and his family. He's been sober almost ten years but his family won't have nothing to do with him. Not even his grandkids. And that's been the hardest because he loves kids."

"Oh."

That afternoon, I loaded my fishing rod, tackle box, and backpack into the man's Volkswagen van and we drove out to our ranch, to the fishpond where I had driven with my grandfather so many times before. The day was hot and the van felt stuffy and awkward at first. But the elderly man seemed happy and asked about school and what I liked to study and the small talk continued on that long gray ribbon of road to the fishpond. And although it was too hot for fishing, we waded through the tallgrass at the edge of the pond casting our lines on the water while water bugs skittered across the water and dragonflies colored the green grass in fitful smudges of blue. We talked now and again and he asked if I knew a particular teacher at my school. I said I did.

"He's my son," he said smiling.

"Yeah, I know him. And," I said, threading a night crawler on my barbed hook, "I go to school with his boys."

He held his smile wide and cast his line on the sunlit water and said nothing. Later, we sat in lawn chairs and drank Pepsis we had packed and munched on peanuts and then called it a day. He had caught one trout and I had caught none. When he dropped me off at the hotel, he shook my hand and thanked me. "I can't tell you how much this meant," he said.

"Yeah. It was fun. We'll have to go again."

"I'd like that."

I grabbed my things and watched him motor out of our parking lot. Little did I know how often we would end up going. Every other Saturday for awhile. Then once a month when the weather was good. One day at school, I saw one of the man's grandchildren. "Hey," I said. "I saw your grandpa last weekend."

He stared at me with a strange look.

"We went fishing."

"Oh," he said. "Yeah, well, we never see him. Gotta go!" He ran off through the crowded hallway and that was the last time it was ever mentioned.

In all those fishing trips our conversations were just as spare as the first one, but the awkwardness was gone. There was solace there, an unmistakable calm between us, as if each of us somehow needed it. The whistling of our lines finding water. The birdsong and the crickets and all the tiny living things that made that whole pond buzz, feverish, a promise whispering back.

21. The Man Missing

At about the same time Dad's green pickup idled back into the parking lot from Alaska, Sherrod returned from Las Vegas to live again with his dad, and my grandfather was rushed to the hospital. I was entering the sixth grade and my grandfather's end seemed imminent. "I don't know if he'll make it," my grandmother had said to me with a quavering voice. "I just don't know." The hospital in Soda Springs had its limits when it came to treating advanced emphysema, and those limits had been reached. It was then decided that he transfer to the hospital in Logan, Utah, some seventy miles south. There were other limits as well. My grandparents did not have insurance. Hospital bills, increasing by the number and in cost, had to be paid in cash. And there were limits to available cash, too. But it was a core philosophy of my grandfather that where limits existed so did alternatives. "You don't have problems," he would famously say. "You have opportunities." Their opportunity came in the form of a doctor who had agreed to accept bulk meat from the café as payment toward their medical expenses. Steaks, chops, cutlets, hamburger, ribs, liver, roasts, and on and on. All of it wrapped in our white butcher paper like

147

Christmas gifts, frozen, and delivered in the driveway of his home just outside of Logan.

You do what you have to do.

Not much more than a week later, my grandfather was released. Everyone at the Enders breathed easier even if he couldn't. It was a narrow escape, we knew, a slice of bought time, and for once, I really began to question what life might be like without him there. Without him on his bedside. Or working at the cash register during the lunch rush. Or washing dishes after the dinner crowd. Or engineering the dumb waiter. Solving a plumbing problem. Laying carpet. Checking people into their rooms. Whatever. But each time the notion firmed up into something discernable, something clear, it blurred and faded just as quickly back into a smudge of abstraction. He had always been there. Always. That was the thing I could not get past.

August pooled on the hot pavement and then disappeared. September leaned against the barley fields shorn of their fruit, harvest-ripe on the warm air. October arrived in the morning, a gathered shroud of frost on the hillsides. And so autumn hung thick in layers of wood smoke and the days grew shorter. This is a ritual time in places like Soda Springs, Idaho. The hills roar with fall color as if they had been set afire. Rifles are cradled in gun racks in pickup trucks. Everyone wears orange, or, for the archers, camouflage. It is hunting season and you can feel it. There is a primal need and the air is scented with its want. And those needs and wants are met with the far-off thud of gun reports, that song echoing in the canyons. The moon, a white belly in the sky. And the blood-smeared grass. The order of things is hastened by the first snow. Deer, elk, moose, mountain lion, and bear are betrayed by their own tracks, where they bedded down the night before, their scat. The first snow reveals in sharp contrast their world to ours, and ours to theirs.

Every year our family made certain that the hunters got their breakfasts and sack lunches. This is how we met the needs of the season. We opened our doors not at the usual six o'clock, but at five. It was a sacrifice that paid off, too, because the café—whose walls were adorned with two antler racks, one elk, one deer—was packed with hunters almost every morning. I remember the Sunday the taxidermist mounted the elk antlers and hung them in the café. He and Dad were talking over coffee. It must have been a strained conversation—the avid hunter and taxidermist talking with Dad who had little use for either endeavor, but I remember wanting to be part of that dialogue. I craned my neck up to that massive six-point rack and said, "Was it a boy or a girl?"

Dad started laughing and shook his head sheepishly. "It was a male, pard. Males have antlers. Females don't."

The taxidermist didn't laugh though. He looked embarrassed. For me. For Dad. For the whole unacceptable thing.

I felt stupid and humiliated and robbed of what I took to be the most essential things, so I moped out of the lobby and disappeared into the apartment.

On those early mornings in the café, white sack lunches—filled with roast beef sandwiches, chips, a banana, and milk or soda—lined the counter. More often than not, I saw this pre-dawn production first hand, because more often than not, it had snowed the night before which meant I was up with the snow blower. But I wanted to be part of that production. I wanted to be the one hunting, not the one serving those who would hunt. But my grandfather was in no condition to take me hunting. Besides, he had all but given up hunting years earlier. Dad refused to go, as did my mother. That left my grandmother who had hunted for years when she and my grandfather still lived on the ranch.

One day that fall, a strange thing happened. Mom stepped into the apartment for a cigarette break and wanted to talk. I had been in my room feeding one of my most recent obsessions: music. My floor was cluttered with music magazines and record jackets. My subscription to *Boy's Life* gave way to a subscription to *Rolling Stone*. Mom had been talking with Becky, one of our waitresses whose husband, Mike, was a deputy sheriff. The subject was guns.

"You know my feelings about guns, Brandon," she began. "So this might come as a bit of a shock to you, but I want you to hear me out." I sat up on my bed.

"Okay."

"I signed you up to be in the NRA."

"What's that?"

"The National Rifle Association."

"Um, okay—"

"Now, I don't want you to think your poor old mother has lost her marbles or anything, but I think it's a good idea." She paused and lit her cigarette.

Her hedging, I thought, had more to do with her feelings on the matter than my own.

"The way things are going anymore, there may come a day when we won't have the right to own guns."

"What do you mean?"

"I mean there may come a time when the government won't allow it, is what I mean."

"Like they'll take them away?"

"Stranger things have happened."

I hadn't considered this as a real possibility before. It seemed strange, movie-like.

"And if anyone knows about this kind of thing, it's Mike. Based on the stuff he's been told at work and everything else, I don't know. It just might happen. I pray it won't, but it could. And this is coming from *me*, someone who detests guns. I hate them. You know that."

"Because of that shooting in the bar?"

She looked right at me. "That—and because of a lot of things. I won't own them. Don't want nothing to do with them." She took a drag from her cigarette and exhaled. "Irregardless, I think we should at least have the *right* to have them. It's in the constitution." We sat for a moment while she took another drag. Finally I shrugged and said, "Okay."

She parked her cigarette in a glass ashtray, removed her glasses, and cleaned them on her shirt. "Grandma said you wanted to go hunting."

I nodded.

"You know I don't like the idea."

I nodded again.

"We don't need the meat, so there isn't a need to go—or at least that's the way I see it." She paused as if to let this thought sink in. "But," she said, "I also understand why you might want to go. So, here's the deal. Grandma said she will take you, but you've got to take hunter's safety first."

"I know. I wanted to."

"That's the rule. Fair?"

I nodded. "Thanks."

"All right. Well, I have to get back at it." She stubbed out her cigarette in the ashtray she had been holding, and left me to my music magazines.

Hunter's Safety was held nightly in the elementary school cafeteria. It was crowded the first night I attended and I was surprised to see so many girls and women there. But as I looked around recognizing most of the faces either from school or the café, my surprise waned. It made sense. This was something you just did—man, woman, child. You learned your way around the mountains and the gunstock. But what I remember most about the class was a movie we watched. As the film fluttered on the projector's spool, the images on the screen frightened me. Shot, perhaps, in the 1960s, the film depicted a hunter lost in the woods. The narrator walked us through the hunter's myriad mistakes. He did not stay put. He did not hug a tree and wait for the rescuers to find him. Instead, he panicked. He started running wildly, foolishly, through heavy drift-snow. He fell in an icy creek. He broke his ankle. And unable to move, he began to sob. His hypothermic state grew so grim, that his mind began to unravel to the point of madness. The situation grew so dire that when his rescuers were finally near at hand he actually hid from them fearing that they were hunting him, that they would kill him. I was horrified.

When I completed Hunter's Safety, my grandmother gave me, as a reward, her hunting rifle, a bolt-action .257 Roberts. It was not a common rifle, but a good one. It was unadorned, its wood stock faded and scratched from use. But it was solid, and sure sighted. So I bought a box of shells and my grandmother and I drove to the shooting range—a wind-blown wash of gravel and scree, achromatic lesions fringed with June grass—for target practice. I was drawn immediately to its power, that authoritative kick. I liked its heft in my hands, and its composition—all wood and metal. And the bolt-action itself—that staccato *shock-chuck-chock* rhythm—was invigorating. There was something about putting a bullet through the paper target and shucking a spent shell that said I had arrived somehow. But as I looked around the range, something felt out of place. I saw fathers with their sons, boys and men and their guns, and there I was with my grandmother. Her cigarettes and thermos of coffee on the metal picnic table. We were conspicuous in that way. We had arrived in a red Volkswagen Rabbit, not a pickup like the others had. Inside, feelings of gratitude and shame fought for expression, and shame surfaced first. I may have seen women and girls at Hunter's Safety, but for some reason the shooting range wasn't the same, and I felt myself shrink with each poor shot I took.

The night before my first hunt I cleaned my rifle. I was delighted by the scent of the gun oil. In fact I don't know if I had ever smelled anything sweeter and surer than the rich scent of a freshly cleaned gun. Before I turned out my light, I set out everything I would need at four thirty in the morning when my grandmother would rouse me for breakfast. I put my boots, coat, orange hat, and wool socks at the foot of my bed, and piled a pair of long johns on my dresser. I propped the rifle in one corner of my room with its muzzle aimed at the skylight and placed the green box of shells on my shelf across the room preventing, I thought, the possibility of their union with the rifle while I slept.

When the call came I was on my feet, but half asleep. I dressed and crossed the dark lobby to the café. My grandmother had just turned on all of the lights. It was a quarter to five. "Go unlock the door and turn the sign around," she said. My mother was at the counter with a cigarette and coffee. She looked at me and laughed. "You need some toothpicks to keep your eyes open?"

"I'm awake," I said as I unlocked the front door and turned the sign from CLOSED to OPEN.

"I see that."

"Have some coffee," my grandmother said.

I was stunned. I had never been offered coffee before. "Really?"

"No!" she said in a gust of sarcasm. "I just said that to make conversation with myself, you ass. Yes, *really*."

I chuckled, pleased by the offer and her usual teasing manner.

"You're getting to be quite the little man, Brandon," my mother said, amused.

I yawned widely and took a stool at the counter. My grandmother got me a cup of coffee and slid a sugar jar at me. "There. You'll probably need that crap." My grandmother took her coffee black and it was her standard drink—morning, noon, and night. Coffee. Not soda. Not juice. Never milk. Not water. Just coffee. In the summer when the sun blazed outside and temperatures shot to a hundred degrees, it was coffee. Hot, black coffee. She was as tough as sagebrush.

A couple of hunters pushed through the door, letting in the frosty draft from outside, and I shook off the chill.

Regular customers, bedecked in orange, these guys wore their hats like Grandpa wore his: cocked to the side. They straddled stools next to me and the tall one, Larry, ribbed me with his elbow and pointed to my coffee. "That'll put hair on your chest."

"That's what they tell me."

"Today is his first hunt," my grandmother said. "Let's hope he don't get buck fever."

"Ah, he'll be fine," Larry said. "As long as he don't shoot like Ed here."

Three more people came in for breakfast. One in the group put his head on the table. The other two were making fun of him. It became clear that he was terribly hung-over and my grandmother, who had their menus, made a joke. "Did we play a little too hard last night?"

"More like a few hours ago."

"Oh, I don't miss those days," my grandmother said.

The man let out a whimper.

One of his friends said to the sick man, "Raise *one* finger if you're going to live, and *two* if you ain't."

He raised three. Everyone laughed. "That can't be good," Larry, the hunter to my side, said and winked.

"Well, I better get those damn pies made," my mother said and stood. She grabbed her coffee, turned to me, and said, "I want to talk to you before you go."

I nodded and took a drink from my overly sweetened coffee.

At a quarter after five, the place was buzzing, and Rose, the morning cook, and Janet, the morning waitress, both had arrived. I would finish my breakfast and we would go, but not before I talked with my mother and heard a litany of her usual cautions and warnings.

Before we left, though, my grandmother reached under the counter, hauled out the pipe wrench, and walked around to the front of the café near the window where the brass radiator stood, and started banging on the pipes. The regular wake-up call to a man staying upstairs. I knew who the man was by sight only. He was a roughneck catching some work at Washington Construction and drove a Ford pickup the color of a school bus. He was tall and had short, dark hair, and his soft dark eyes and face held an expression as if he were always on the verge of apologizing. I never spoke to him but I always nodded when I saw him in the lobby or café or on his way into the bar. Each time my grandmother knocked the wrench against the steam pipes, the hung-over man winced and moaned while his friends clapped at the show. Then she stopped and we all listened. Suddenly there came the answer, a clanking sound from above.

"He's up," my grandmother reported.

"Whether he likes it or not, by God," Larry said and chuckled.

When the café was in order and running on its own feet, my grandmother gave me the signal and we set out. We were going with Marge, one of her closest friends. Marge, a tall, broad-shouldered woman with bright orange hair, owned a hair salon and a police scanner so she could keep abreast on all the shenanigans in Soda Springs. But here it gets complicated. Marge was my grandfather's ex-wife. Years later, when Marge remarried, the two couples dined out together, traveled together, and hunted together. Nothing about their entangled relationship struck them as odd as it struck most people. Besides, my grandmother and Marge were friends through school and they did not see any sense of ending that just because they had been married to the same man.

I was still partly groggy as the headlights of Marge's pickup truck cut through the weak blue light of morning, and flattened out on the dirt road that wound like a ribbon of graphite through the humped fields of the ranch. The hunting was good, my grandmother knew, in the draws and slot canyons, above the fields. Soon we turned off the main road and aimed the truck toward a hollow where we jounced along a set of semi-frozen ruts. "Here," my grandmother said and Marge cut the lights. We sat for a moment in the truck drinking coffee from a green Stanley Thermos while the heater purred at our feet and the sun fell through a slit in the sky at our backs.

"We ought to wait just a little longer for more sun, so it's legal," my grandmother said. She pulled the cigarette lighter from the metal dash and put the glowing orange coils to the end of her Bel-Air menthol, and passed it to Marge who did the same. Our rifles were cradled in the gun rack in the rear window: my .257, Marge's

.270, and my grandmother's .30/30. I looked down at my boots. One of my laces had come untied. My stomach swirled and knotted, pitched, and heaved. And when we finally swung the heavy truck doors open, I slipped and stumbled and jammed the barrel of my rifle into the ground. When I reached down to recover the gun, my box of shells slipped from my coat pocket and spilled on the ground. Instantly, tears welled in my eyes and my lip began to quiver.

Everything was wrong.

About an hour later I had settled into my perch on a craggy outcrop that jutted out from a hillside. Below, the hill cupped a stand of aspens in a coulee. I was high up toward the ridge so I could see most anything that moved in or out of that grove. Marge and my grandmother stayed near the truck parked out of my line of fire. Should I brush anything out, they would have a clean shot of it. With my pocketknife, I whittled a thin spear from a black hawthorn and set about cleaning the granules of earth clogging the muzzle of my gun. I drew the barrel to my face, peered in, and blew. And though I hadn't loaded the gun, I checked the chamber two and three times to be certain. I thought I had cleaned it well enough to shoot but couldn't be sure. What if there was just enough dirt in one of the riflings that it jammed the gun and the rifle exploded in my hands? While I stewed on the images of my own death, I heard the heavy-footed clomp and snort of deer in the pocket of aspens below. Through the trees I caught a flash of gray. Then it emerged full-bodied and as big as dawn itself. A four-point thirty yards below me. It looked up, nose steaming, and turned back to browsing. I drew a bead, switched off my safety, and sat there. I was paralyzed. I couldn't do it. Just like that, the buck jumped through the brush and was gone.

We drove home without a kill and I listened to Marge and my grandmother swap stories about this hunt or that. Stories of getting the truck stuck. Of poaching under the swinging beam of a spotlight. Of outwitting the Fish & Game wardens. They were stories from another world, and I just sat there between these two

156

women listening with my hands pinned between my knees, knowing that no story would come from this hunt.

I had not thought about the man who had ordered a wake-up call on the morning of my first hunt until he had gone missing. He, too, had risen early that morning to hunt. But when he did not return to work the next day, the discussion of his getting lost in the brushy mountains grew more and more harried with each passing hour. The Caribou County Search and Rescue had assembled and the Enders Café provided their meals in another row of white paper lunch sacks and thermoses of steaming hot coffee (in the summer we would do the same, but on a much larger scale, for firefighters and hotshot crews). My grandmother wished them luck. "Bring him back," she said. Outside it was cold and a storm front loomed at the west. It would arrive by nightfall. Fresh snow would erase his tracks. In the café, men recalled stories of lost hunters, those who never made it back, whose skeletal remains—strewn by chance predators—weren't discovered until the spring thaw. These were the stories you could learn from.

That night while the storm howled over my skylight, I tossed and turned, haunted by the film I had seen in Hunter's Safety. My mind kept casting our guest, the lost man, in the lead role of the deranged hunter in the film. And then something unexpected happened. I began sobbing uncontrollably. I felt stupid and sentimental with my head resting on my wet pillow.

They found the man the next morning. Hypothermic, frostbitten, and exhausted, but otherwise intact. He stayed on at the Enders for a few weeks after that, and each time I saw him in the café or lobby I had made it a habit of saying hello. He returned my sudden niceties with a smile or a nod. I wanted to get to know him and hear him tell the story of that hunt, but like the rest, he would also check out, and vanish.

All the while my grandfather's condition worsened and though we didn't know it at the time, he would be taken from us before that hunting season drew to a close.

22. A New Year

Winter barreled headlong into the days of failing light, and the cold scoured the air of what little water it held. The day after Christmas, my grandfather was again rushed to the hospital in Logan, Utah. My grandmother came home a few days later to pack some necessities and I joined her in the return to Logan. My mother sent a note to school. "You need to be with Grandma," she said. "Go."

The drive was quiet as we hummed along a wavy ribbon of ice-covered highway. Heavy gusts blew snow across the car's hood and churned on the road before us like whirlpools. My mother and dad stayed behind to attend to the hotel and café. We would call when we arrived. We would call if anything "changed." Something had already changed, though. Our language had changed. Everything uttered was suspended, conditional. There was a resigned tone to it all, and I tried to match my own words to those that surrounded me.

We checked into our hotel room and stayed long enough to use the restroom before we reported to the hospital ICU. The hospital room was cramped and half lit. Tubes and wires sprouted from his wrists and the full-faced oxygen mask in great tendrils, snaking their way into monitors and machines. "Hi, Grandpa," I said at his bedside, but he did not reply.

"Can he hear me?"

"Sure, he can hear you," my grandmother said. "He knows you're here."

The night before, he had slipped into a coma. It was unlikely, the doctor had said, that he would come out of it. But, the doctor was quick to add, he was not suffering. So that had changed. My grandmother made a battery of phone calls. To my mother who would tell my aunt LaNae. To my uncles Jerry, and the twins, Doug and Dallas. To my grandfather's sisters who would call his brother, Ted. To friends. And all the while, I sat bedside, numb, watching images skate across the television screen in that cold blue glow. Later I wandered the hospital, hitting the snack machine or cafeteria just to break up the hours. And when I passed through the ICU wing I stopped where I could put my face to a wall of windows that peered outside. Gray slush filled the streets like waste and a winter fog—common in Logan—had settled across the valley. It was impenetrable. I touched my forehead to the large pane and its iciness sent a shiver through me.

The next night I counted down the New Year on a digital alarm clock in the hotel room by myself in a self-conscious whisper: . . . *three, two, one*. My grandmother had called from the hospital room and said she would be fifteen minutes or so longer. "Some New Year," she said. She was exhausted.

"Yeah. No kidding."

I had come from a hotel to stay in a hotel. Nothing was permanent. The digital clock's red numbers, illuminated and blockish, were a minute or so faster than the television, which I had turned to the Salt Lake Channel. Time seemed to have arrived more quickly where I was than in Salt Lake City, as if the inevitable was closer at hand than we thought. I watched the throngs of people cheer on Temple Square and wondered what it must be like to be there. Other channels replayed the ball dropping in the Big Apple. And I wondered what New York was like, too. But those places and those people seemed like a fairy tale, some intangible fantasyland. It was 1986 and I wondered what the year would promise or what else it would take away.

I stood and stepped to the hotel window and drew back the drapes. I could feel a draft as I stared into the half-empty parking lot glazed with ice. The fog had thickened and was luminescent in the glow of the streetlamps. I tried to feel something like sadness or sorrow or pity or anger, but felt only guilt for feeling none of these things, so I left the window and crawled into bed and shut my eyes.

Within two days, the family had arrived. Uncles, aunts, my mother and dad. Friends came, too. The help looked after the café and hotel. "It's only a matter of time, now," my grandmother kept saying. That time came in the evening on January 4th. It had been a quiet day. The fog had lifted a little and the snow made the day unusually bright. That morning my uncle Dallas and I wandered down to the cafeteria to get some breakfast. I ordered Pop-Tarts and he ordered a bagel and cream cheese.

"What's a beagle?" I asked.

He chuckled. "You mean *bagel*? It's like a roll, sort of. They're good. You should try one."

"That's okay," I said, sticking to my crumbling pastries.

The things you remember. The strange things you remember.

Then my grandfather flat-lined that evening. The piercing sound drew three nurses in the room, and sent my mother out, head in her hands, bawling. I was on the floor near the bed watching television. I sat up, dazed. Then I stood, and when I glanced at my grandmother she looked like she had been slugged. I don't remember anything after that. Not leaving the hospital. Not going back to the hotel. Not the drive home to our own hotel. Nothing.

"I want a nice headstone for him," my grandmother said later in those scrambled hours that come with planning a funeral. "I

160

don't care what it costs. I want the best." Everyone had gathered in the apartment. There was much to do, so much to sort out. I was excluded from much of it because I was still considered a boy. Paperwork and the will and god knows what else. In the fuss of it all, my grandmother looked at me and said, "You're going to need something nice to wear. For the funeral. Go to Blocks, get what you like, and tell them to charge it."

Blocks was an upscale department store by Soda Springs standards, which meant you could buy your church clothes there. Or, in this case, funeral clothes. We weren't a dress-up family. My grandmother wore basic blouses and slacks always, and my grandfather wore nondescript slacks or khakis and button-down shirts. That was as dressy as it got. But my mother, dad, and I kicked around in jeans. We didn't go to church and had never, in my memory, attended an event that required clothing outside of the everyday T-shirt and Levi's.

Word spread through town like wind. It wasn't long before I got a call from B.J.

"How's it going?" he asked.

"My grandpa died."

"I know. My old man told me. The folks wanted me to see if you guys need anything, or anything."

"I think we're okay," I said looking around the room at everyone who had gathered. My Uncle Doug had a photo album and they were doing the *remember when?* thing. "Hey, you want to do something?"

"Sure. Like what?"

"I dunno. Anything. I need to get out of here."

"Let's go to Double Kwik."

"Hold on a sec." I cupped the mouthpiece with the palm of my hand. "Mom can I go to Double Kwik with B.J.?"

Doug looked up from the photo album. "Who's B.J.?"

"Beaver's boy," my grandmother interjected.

"No kidding . . . How is old Beaver these days?"

"Mom . . ."

"Beaver is Beaver."

"*Mom!*"

"What?"

"Can I hang out with B.J.?"

"Where?"

"Double Kwik, *God!*"

"I want you home by six o'clock. We're all going to eat."

I uncupped the phone. "It's cool."

"I'll see you in like ten."

Double Kwik was a convenient store and gas station that sat across the highway from our junior high school. Its proximity made it our hang out. They had a game room, nachos, candy, pop, and condoms. Everything we would need or fancied we would need. Plus we liked to bullshit with Robert, a twenty-year-old clerk with dark shaggy hair who worked the afternoon shift. We got to know Robert when we would hit Double Kwik after wrestling practice. And perhaps the best thing about Robert is that he would sell us cigarettes. But if Robert wasn't working, Brenda was. We all had a thing for Brenda. She was single, in her late twenties, had long blonde hair, and wore tight jeans. I am sure I wasn't the only one in our group of friends who entertained thoughts of doing Brenda. With Brenda it was a constant flirt show. We jockeyed for the best position as sole receiver of her attentions that we took, in that adolescent way, to be affections. And often I would win this favor as she asked me to help her with this or that around the store.

When B.J. knocked at the door, I grabbed my coat, and slipped out. The day was cold and four-foot snow banks lined the center of all the city streets. Double Kwik was three blocks from the hotel. Our pace was hurried, and we hunkered into the gray light. The snow squeaked underfoot. "Sorry about your grandpa, man."

I shrugged. "It happens."

"How much money you got?" he asked changing tack.

"Enough for a few games and a Coke."

"Cool. Me, too."

Halfway there, B.J. looked around and then left the road cutting through a field of snow by the railroad tracks. "What are you doing?"

"Cigarette."

"Cool."

He was heading for one of three abandoned wooden grain silos. You could shimmy through a small opening at the base of them and they were empty save a sprinkling of mouse scat, bird shit, and the occasional torn page from a *Playboy*. But they made for a good hideout. Inside the silo we sparked up our cigarettes and tried to shake off the cold. I craned my neck upward. The ceiling was nearly fifty feet high. Light poured through every crack in the old building and through one major hole in the ceiling, which explained a small, dirty patch of snow in the one corner of the hexagonal silo. The walls were riddled with graffiti and so was the cement floor.

"I bet people have bumped uglies in here," B.J. said, looking around.

"Totally."

"You know it wouldn't be half bad. To bang a chick here."

"If you swept it up and brought some blankets and shit," I said and took another drag.

We talked for awhile in the chill watching our breath and the smoke pass through the shafts of wan light while the cigarettes burned down.

B.J. looked at me. "You about done?"

I nodded. "One more drag."

We dropped the smokes to the cement, ground them into the floor with our sneakers, and slipped out of the crawlspace back into the snow, and slugged our way through the cold.

163

23. Requiem

Because we were Mormons on paper and not in practice, my grandfather's funeral was held in a Mormon church. It was the only church we knew. The chapel was filled and I was stunned by how many people were there, people whose faces I recognized and many more whose faces I didn't. Three rows back the whole Weaver family crowded a pew. I picked out B.J. and we exchanged nods. They weren't a dress-up family either and it was strange to see them making that kind of effort. The boys in button-down shirts and clean jeans. Their sister in a dress. Beaver in a sport coat over a western-style shirt and his best dress shoes. And his mother in makeup and a dress.

I scanned my family, too, who looked miserable in polyester and in church, their faces washed of blood by grief. My grandmother was flanked by family, propped up, this widow, this frail shell of a person. My cousin, Jade, dabbed his puffy eyes. How is he crying when I cannot? I wondered. I turned my sober gaze to the pew in front of me and concentrated on the whorls and the knots that made up the surface of that polished wood. And I listened. I listened to the anecdotes, the stories told by family and friends, stories that tried, and succeeded varyingly, to lift the despair. The story about when he built his own car when he was in high school. "It was the damndest-looking thing, but it *ran*." Stories of lambing in the spring. Stories of helping those in need. Of being a rancher, a businessman, a soldier, a philanthropist, a father. I took each story in hopes that I would never lose them. The best stories I knew had come from him and now he was gone. But despite that ceremony, the blanched faces and the ruddy ones, too, and despite the casket, that ominous box in the front blazing with flowers, despite all that, his absence seemed strikingly temporary. It was as if he had just left the room, and he would step back in and call it all off. Perhaps that is why I could not find the tears. And when no tears came, I tried to think of all the saddest things in my life to that point, reasoning perhaps, that cumulative sadness might usher in the flood this occasion seemed to demand.

If the funeral was a glum event, the burial was worse. The weather did not cooperate and the temperature dropped below zero. The sky and the land looked like one empty wash of white, their contact points obliterated out of perspective. We could have just as easily been standing ankle-deep in the sky with headstones jutting out instead of stars—each marking things long since gone.

The wind cut through my white cotton slacks and my teeth chattered uncontrollably. But it was during the twenty-one gun salute—when that cluster of veterans shot their weapons into the emptiness—that my grandmother broke. Those relentless reports roaring over this gnarled and cruel landscape. Her legs buckled and Dad caught her. All gazes shot her way. But those shots kept coming louder and louder, and that rifle fire, that ceaseless, maddening rifle fire.

24. Visitors

Not long after the funeral, a woman with several children showed up in the café asking first to talk to the owner, and second, with Bud Schrand. This was a page from Dad's past standing in the Enders Café: an ex-wife, his two daughters, Crystal and Valerie, and a handful of other children who did not belong to him. "I need more child support," she said loud enough for customers to hear. "As you can see."

Everyone stole glances. Paused over their soup or cups of coffee. Dabbed their mouths with napkins.

"Okay," he said. "But now is not the time or place." He moved them from the café into the lobby.

I was not there and learned of their arrival the next day, long after they had gone. My mother had mentioned their visit casually while she operated a whirring meat-slicer. I stared as she turned a large ham into a stack of thinly sliced sandwich meat. I couldn't fully process what that encounter meant and felt caught somewhere between resentment and wonder. On the one hand their presence, which hung in the air ghost-like, seemed threatening, as if they could lure my dad away. That he might look around him, around this place, this crumbling hotel, and say, sorry, but I've got to go. That his green pickup would idle out of the parking lot and never come back. I feared part of his past. I feared his daughters, that otherness about them that claimed, by blood, something I felt was rightfully mine. We may have shared the same last name, but I knew him. They didn't. Besides, he was the only father I had ever known, the only one whose face was clear to me. But I also couldn't help but wonder about other things. If they showed up at the Enders Hotel looking for their father, wouldn't it stand to reason that my father might show up looking for me? And so I wondered while my mother finished slicing the ham, and while she moved on to another topic wholly removed from the one spinning in my head.

25. The Hand Out

Like so many other times when I felt the need to vanish, I would steal away into the pages of a book, hoping that the book might make some sense of the world as I knew it. I read in the café at the yellow lunch counter, scanning lines as I spun around on a barstool, with a straw in my mouth. "Watcha reading?" one of the waitresses would ask, and I would tell them while trying to sound uninterested or bored even with the book in my hands.

Not long after the funeral, my seventh grade English teacher, Ms. Clack—a big-breasted woman from New Hampshire who said *idear* instead of *idea*—passed out copies of S. E. Hinton's *The Outsiders*. "This is a book about class. About the haves and the have nots. I want you to think about the title as you read. I really think you'll enjoy it." On this last note, she shot me a glance as I thumbed through the paperback. The book was about three brothers who were trying to get on with life in the wake of their parents' tragic death. But it was more than that. It was the story of social injustice, of sacrifice, of brotherhood, loyalty, and friendship. Tough kids with switchblades and long hair carving out a place in a tough world. They were the Greasers and their world clashed with the Socs's. It felt like the book had been written for me, its pages spilling forth all the secrets of this dark and strange world, and it was a world I wished to inhabit.

The only class I was passing was English, and that with only a tepid B-average. I was failing science, social studies, math, and history, making matters at home unbearable.

Dad had a litany of loathsome chores he held in store for when I committed one trespass or another. Usually I had to clean out around the Dumpsters, the ones Trapper Jim had pinched from, in the parking lot. A solid hedge of yellow Harrison roses stood behind the trash cans: thirty feet long, five feet deep, and six feet tall. This brambled wall of thorns seemed to swipe errant trash into its prickly clutches. So when a poor report card came home, I could count on hours of beating that hedge with a rake in fits of rage, and how it always won; how its branches and thorns grabbed the tines of the rake leaving me all the more outraged as I tried to tug the rake free: "Dirty rotten son of a bitch!" We were sworn enemies, that godforsaken hedge and I.

That was one job.

Others varied. Sweep the basement. Organize the tool room. Clean the garage. Each project designed to consume entire afternoons. And while I drew a wage for my regular chores—making French fries, cutting meat, taking out boxes, stocking shelves, and refilling the water softeners with rock salt—the punishment jobs went without pay.

Inevitably I fell behind on my chores. And I cut corners. Nothing angered Dad more than a less than perfectly executed job. His expectations had no ceiling and were known only to him. The goal of perfection, it goes without saying, was a moving target. When I did my best, I fell short. So I reasoned, in that maladjusted way of teenagers, that I should do the bare minimum because the outcome was very nearly the same. The same derision. The same mocking, incisive phrases: "Do I have to hold your hand, Brandon? Huh? It's always a half-assed effort from you. While the rest of the world works for a living, here's Mister Big Shot running around with his hand out."

The hand out. That was his favorite thing to harp on. Nothing boiled his blood like the times I asked for spending money. Nothing.

The day I cut the biggest corner was a Sunday. I had been cutting meat all afternoon. Feeding ribbons of meat through the grinder to make Swiss steak. Slicing a beef liver for a dinner special. Grinding fat into renderings. Trouble was, the work had backed up, and B.J. and Sherrod wanted to hang out. I knew I had at least two hours of work ahead of me, so I decided to shorten it. I took half the meat on the tray—half the steak set aside to be cubed into chicken-fried steaks—and threw it in the Dumpster. I had simply trashed quality grass-feed beef—something on the order of four to five pounds—so I could duck out with my friends.

I was in my room getting ready to take off when all of a sudden I was knocked to the floor and the whole side of my head was ringing. I looked up, dazed. It was Dad and he had somehow discovered the meat I had scattered in the Dumpster. He hit me again, another blow to the side of my head. All I could hear was a shrill ring while his mouth moved. And then I turned just in time for him to hit the back of my neck. The blow sent a shockwave down my spine and for a split second my entire body went numb. I was filled with terror and a squall of anger all at once.

Later I found my mother in their apartment and appealed to her for sympathy. "He hit me in the neck! I mean I could have been *paralyzed*!"

"Oh, don't be dramatic," she said and lit a cigarette. "What the hell were you thinking, anyway? Throwing away all that meat? Jesus, Brandon. If Grandpa were here, he'd be so disappointed in you."

I had no defense and so I hung my head, and sulked. I felt hollowed by shame. "He's not even my real dad," I muttered and started to walk away.

170

"Don't even go there, Brandon. Don't you dare."

"Whatever." I stepped outside and looked north. Monsanto had dumped a fresh cauldron of slag, and the sky beheld a coppery tincture that waned and grayed as I stood there in the shadow of the hotel.

26. Apprentice

One afternoon I was sent out of science class for disrupting the teacher. Down the hall a classroom door opened and out stepped an eighth grader, David Hale, a hulkish kid I took to be something of a preppy. I looked up as we were the only two in the hallway. He approached and then, as if nothing could have been more natural, he stood on my shins, grinding his weight into my legs and smirking. It felt like my legs were going to snap under his mass. Then he stepped off and started walking away. I grit my teeth, stood, and—with tears dancing at the edges of my eyes—I pulled my butterfly knife from my back pocket, and backed him into the wall. His smirk evaporated and he stood there blinking, wide-eyed and dumb.

"You fat fuck! You want this, you fuck? Do it again, and you'll get some."

"Jesus. I didn't mean anything by it," he said, stammering.

"Do it again," I said, meaning it both as a threat and warning. "I fucking dare you."

"All right, I'm sorry, *God*!"

At that moment I had become my dad, or a kid from a novel,

or anyone of the restless men who stayed with us at the Enders Hotel.

I had become Vic.

I let him go out of the reach of the knife but not my gaze, and when he rounded the corner, I started bawling. I slumped against the wall and slid to the floor and cried until the bell rang, burying my face into my denim jacket sleeve. At the bell, I disappeared into the bathroom where I could cool down.

It wasn't the only time I had gone after someone after injuring me. That previous fall I was on the sidewalk in front of the hotel when two kids from school, Todd and Tyler—kids I knew well enough—approached me with their freckly faces and smiles. "Hey, Brandon," they had said. "What's up?"

"Nothing."

Something was amiss but I couldn't read the situation, those too-wide smiles, those hands behind their backs. The next thing I knew, Todd had grabbed my arms and Tyler lit a smoke bomb and threw it down the back of my shirt. My flesh blistered on contact and it felt like water running down my spine. The whole thing lasted only seconds before the bomb burned through my shirt and fell out onto the sidewalk in front of the bar and poured its green smoke around me. I charged into the building, crossed the lobby, and into the apartment where I peeled off the burnt shirt and wailed on the couch.

"What the hell is the matter?" my grandmother had said.

"My back!" It's all I could say. After she attended to the burns, I walked, clench-jawed, into the closet, grabbed the .257 deer rifle, loaded it, and, before she could stop me, ran outside looking for Todd and Tyler.

Had I seen them, I would have killed them.

It must have been a sight. A red-eyed shirtless teen standing on an Idaho Main Street in the shadow of the Enders Hotel gripping a high-powered deer rifle, his finger on the trigger, consumed with that hot want of blood we call revenge. But before I could depress the trigger and discharge a round into god knows what or whom, my grandmother pulled me into the hotel and got the gun away. "I ought to slap your goddamn face off. So they burned your back. It was a stupid prank. A stunt. Something *you* might have done, by the way. And you grab a gun? Jee-sus Christ. Grow up."

27. The Man on the Stairs

I was trying to grow up and that was precisely the problem. How easy it is to misread the world of adults, and the mistakes of men you take as lessons to be learned. Coming home late one evening, I hit the sidewalk in front of the café just as the sky shot orange from a slag pour, and I ducked in. Inside it was warm and dinner customers cluttered the tables. Behind me the brass radiators clanked away their labored songs of steam and heat, and the peppery scents of grilled chops and burgers wafted from the kitchen. My stomach growled and I stepped back into the kitchen to order some dinner. Cheeseburger deluxe. Always. It was my standard. Fries and a Coke. At my stool, I unzipped my duffel bag, which held my wrestling uniform, a batch of unfinished homework, and my copy of *The Outsiders*. I fished out the book and fanned the pages to my dog-ear. Pony Boy and Johnny were on the run. I read page after page as I sucked down my Coke through a straw and oscillated on the bar stool. I continued to read over my cheeseburger and fries. This book was different because for the first time I was consciously aware, hyperaware even, of the author behind the story. That someone had written this book, hung these sentences together, and envisioned the scope of the story was, to my way of thinking, genius. S. E. Hinton, Ms. Clack had informed us, was young when she wrote the book. Very young. "In fact," she had said, "it started as an assignment she had in school."

I was floored.

After cleaning my plate, wiping the last smudge of ketchup from the dish with the remaining French fry, I dumped the plate and cup into the gray bus tub at the end of the counter, zipped up my duffel, and headed for the apartment. But when I entered the dimly lit lobby I caught my breath when I saw a man lying on the stairway. He was either asleep or dead, I didn't know which. I stopped to see if I could detect any movement, to see if I could hear him breathing, but I couldn't. So I continued to the apartment door and shut it quietly behind me.

Inside, Dad was doing bookwork in my grandfather's place. Just beyond the living room—in which my bedroom was located and portioned off with bamboo dividers—was an office space with a chair, desk, bureau, filing cabinet, and safe. This was the center of the business, and Dad had taken over. My grandfather had in fact been training him before his health took its final turns, sensing, perhaps, the inevitability of the situation. And that sound of the ten-key calculator churning out its script of numbers seemed ever present.

I told Dad about the man on the stairs.

"Did you recognize him?"

"No."

He nodded and grabbed his coffee cup and stood. "Let's see what the deal is," he said, patting his shirt pocket as if he were looking for something.

In the lobby Dad approached the man in the half light easily and cautiously, as if he might be booby-trapped. I hung back by the desk. "Hey, pard," Dad said. And then he tried it louder. No response. Finally he shook the man's shoulder and this kind of prodding elicited only a groan. "*Hey*," he tried again. "We can't have you here on the stairs, pard. Understand?"

More prodding and shaking and then finally, "If you don't move it, I'm calling the cops."

"What's wrong with him?" I asked.

"Too much to drink."

I nodded. The man looked too young not to have a place to go. Something about his frayed jeans and flannel shirt and ratty tennis shoes told me that he did not, in fact, have any other place other than those stairs right at that moment. He mumbled something, flailed a loose arm in Dad's direction, and turned to his other side.

"I guess I have no choice," Dad said and I followed him back into the apartment where he dialed the police.

I paced the lobby a few times waiting for the police to arrive, pretending I had things to attend to in the café and in the apartment and back and forth. I wanted to see what was going to happen. In what seemed like a matter of minutes, the officer dispatched was on the man with his nightstick. While Dad worked over the ten-key, the cop worked over the man while I watched from behind the lobby desk, ducking so I couldn't be seen in the officer's periphery. I shuddered the first time the stick made contact with the man's legs. Winced the second time. Felt my jaw clench on the third, fourth, fifth strikes to the man's body. I was sure the commotion would have drawn attention from the bar or the café or from Dad, but no one came to this man's rescue, least of all me. The cop was breathing hard and I wanted to bolt but didn't dare. The man groaned and cried, "Stop, stop" and "Okay, okay." But the cop only answered the pleas with another barrage of strikes. The entire encounter likely lasted only a minute or two, but it felt elongated, as if it had been stretched out over hours. All I could do was hunker down in the shadow of the lobby desk and clutch my knees to my beating chest.

28. The Man in the Phone Booth

When I saw a man loading a revolver in our lobby phone booth, I just kept walking straight for the apartment door. My chest tightened and tingled and I was certain I would be shot because I had seen him and what he was doing. I had seen his long unkempt hair. The black pistol. The quick glance he shot in my direction. What would it feel like to be shot in the back? I waited for it as I kept walking toward the French doors that led to the apartment. I turned the crystal doorknob casually but quickly and stepped inside and shut the door behind me. I was trembling. My mother and grandmother were in the café and Dad was at the desk doing more bookwork. "There's a man," I started. "In the phone booth. And I think he's got a gun."

"You think?"

"Yeah. I mean, I saw it—I think."

He straightened his back and placed his mechanical pencil in his shirt pocket. "Okay," he said. "I'll go talk to him. You stay here." He started toward the French doors through which we could only make out ghostly shadows and splotches of light. He paused and turned around. "You're sure he had a gun?"

I nodded.

He picked up the phonebook, flipped through its pages, and dialed a number on a beige rotary unit. It was the police. He told them the situation, hung up, and looked at me. "Just in case." Then he stepped out the door and closed it behind him.

Almost all the doors in the Enders Hotel required skeleton keys including my grandparents' apartment. I shut out the living room light and squatted at the door where I could peer through the skeleton keyhole, my chest pounding wildly. But all I could make out from this limited viewpoint was Dad by the lobby desk, his hands out, palms facing the phone booth. He was talking but I couldn't make out what he was saying. Then he dropped his hands and put them in his pockets. I exhaled. They kept talking and then a police officer entered the lobby and the three of them were talking, and the police officer took the man away and out the lobby doors. When Dad came back in, I said, "Well?"

He chuckled sheepishly. "I feel bad for him."

"Why?"

"Just a young guy all busted up over his ex. He wasn't really going to do anything. Maybe just get her attention. But now he's in a bit of trouble with Bugtussle's finest."

"Oh."

"You did the right thing, though. I'm proud of you."

"For what?"

"For not panicking, and coming straight to me. You handled it well. I don't think your mother would have been as cool headed."

"Probably not."

We both laughed, although I laughed because if I hadn't, I would have bawled and gotten all blubbery like I did anytime he said he was proud of me.

29. The Waitress

After *The Outsiders*, Ms. Clack passed around another book called *Shane*. It was some cowboy book and I could not have been less interested. My copy was battered and dusty and the pages' edges were dyed blue like many of the westerns my grandfather used to read. The book made it home and there it sat in my room buried beneath a heap of junk, ignored and unread.

Shortly after Ms. Clack distributed the books, she was attacked by a dog. It was a strange and troubling bit of news. The attack was severe, we were told, but she would recover with time. Substitutes would finish out the spring term. I tried to imagine the struggle, the dog taking her down on a sidewalk under a clear sky. The whole scenario reminded me of a scar on my mother's arm, ridged and as wide and long as your thumb. She, too, had been attacked by a dog, but when she was a girl. I had imagined that scene too. That dog's will to hold on, and the girl's fight to flee. In my mind's eye, I see a fence and a gate that has swung open. The dog belonged behind that fence and had gotten out. So whenever Mom would light a cigarette, I would see that scar across the underside of her forearm, and the whole terrible attack would replay itself in my imagination.

Our first substitute teacher was Mrs. Lawrence, a large, loud woman with dark frizzy hair and large glasses. She was a no-guff sub who came with a reputation of cruelty. She wasn't cruel, of course, but in the substitute teacher mythology of seventh graders, her story figured prominently as the Goliath of all subs. She had subbed for years, drove the school bus on occasion, and worked odd jobs around town.

During that spring term when she was subbing for Ms. Clack, she was also picking up a nightshift as waitress at the Enders Café. When I told this to Sherrod and B.J., their response was unison: "Oh, *God*!"

"I know! It's like I can't get away from the bitch."

"That sucks, man."

"It fucking totally sucks."

But for whatever reason, Mrs. Lawrence liked me. And while she hedged her attentions toward me in the classroom, she was a different person in the café. She thought I was the stuff. This was mostly because of my grandmother, whom she adored. "One of the best women I've ever met," she had said under her breath one night while refilling mustard bottles. "Tough, too. You don't want to mess with her." She winked and I nodded and dabbed my mouth with napkin.

"Tell me about it."

Of course, I mentioned none of this to B.J. and Sherrod.

Her apparent fondness for me did not change my decided aversion to the musty copy of *Shane* lost somewhere in my bedroom, however. I wasn't about to crack that thing. Who cared about gunfights and the small western towns settled at the edge of perpetual sunsets? Not me. I had finished reading *The Outsiders* a second time and checked the card catalogue at school for HINTON, S. E., and was surprised to find several titles. The first I plucked from the shelves was *Rumble Fish*. It was the strangest and coolest book I had ever read. Rusty James, the novel's protagonist, had become my new hero. He typified cool. Meanwhile, Mrs. Lawrence warned of a looming test on *Shane*. I had aced the test on *The Outsiders* and knew, fully knew—and did not care—that I would flunk the upcoming test.

But that was to change.

One night in the café while I was finishing my cheeseburger deluxe at the counter, Mrs. Lawrence toweled down the bar in front of me, then pulled something from her apron pocket. It was a blue sheet of paper folded in thirds. "This will help on Friday," she had said without making eye contact. My stomach lurched.

"Okay."

I dumped my dishes in the gray bus tub as I always had, and nearly sprinted to the apartment where I could unfold the blue slip of paper in private. When I did, my heart pounded. It was the test on *Shane* and it included all the *complete* answers, referencing page numbers and everything. I could not believe my eyes. It was unthinkable. I was stunned. No, I was beyond stunned. I was angry.

In spite of my anger, I spent the next four days memorizing the test, word for word, and underlining coordinating passages as the test was "open book." But I kept that blue sheet a secret and never once breathed a word of it to anyone. Not to B.J., not to Sherrod, no one. And when Friday arrived, I walked into English class, took my seat, and looked out the window. The day was bright and clear and the snow was finally melting under the warm rush of spring. I felt good. And when Mrs. Lawrence handed out the stack of tests, I went to work with my jaw clenched. I was the first to hand in the test and I strolled back to my desk and turned to the pages of *Rumble Fish*.

From that point forward, any time Mrs. Lawrence subbed, I would act out and push the limits, knowing that something existed between us. This was my tacit retaliation. *Go on. Send me to the office, bitch. Let's see where it gets you. I dare you.*

30. Father to Son

I seldom saw any two members of my family together. The building was large enough to get lost in—four stories (including the
basement) and well over one hundred rooms. When my mother
was in the kitchen it meant my grandmother was napping. When
my mother took her nap, Dad was in the walk-in cutting meat. And
when he wasn't cutting meat, or making lists, or running numbers
on the ten-key, he was away on a Union job.

And I avoided all of them at all cost, as teenagers are wont to
do. My grandfather's absence still haunted the hallways of that
place. My grandmother must have felt it, too, because one day she
gave me her bedroom. She took down the bamboo dividers in the
living room, bought a hide-a-bed, and slept in the living room.
Sleeping behind their bedroom door where her husband's scent
was still strong on the linens was too much to bear. Grief sent her
from that room, and sent me in. "You need your own room," she
reasoned. "It's important that you have privacy." I didn't see it as a
gesture of survival on her part, only a token of generosity. She also
started a new restoration project upstairs. All the wood needed
treatment. Sanding and staining. New carpet in the hallways, too.

New lighting. New wallpaper. New everything. She bought a new car.

She was starting over.

Sometimes my mother busied herself with side projects like typing English papers for Frankie, Rose's son. He wrote them long hand and dropped the notebook pages off at the café after school. Rose paid my mother some small amount of money for the trouble, and she enjoyed—despite her false complaints—doing it. "I don't mind," she would say. "Besides, I loved English in school." I remember going over to their small, smoke-filled apartment and stepping inside to see her sitting on the floor with an ashtray and cigarette. Her electric Smith Corona humming patiently before her on a small end table. Sheaves of paper here and there. A bottle of Wite-Out. Crumpled attempts opening like flowers near the trash bin.

Although he would have never showed it outwardly, my dad was affected, too, by my grandfather's death. They had become comrades in the quiet crusade against the government. They received *The Searchlight Newsletter*, a pamphlet from an extremist Freeman-like faction buried somewhere in the west. Arm yourselves, the newsletter would declare. The end is near. It offered tips for survival in the new apocalypse. My dad bought guns despite my mother's protest. One day he said, "I want to show you something." I followed him into his bedroom and he opened his nightstand drawer and exhumed a heavy black pistol, a .38 Special. "I want you to know it's here. But I also want you to know that I've never fired it. I got it from a guy who owed me some money. I don't even know if it is safe to shoot. But I want you to know it's here. Just in case."

"Okay."

"And something else." He put the gun back in the drawer and pulled a tin of tobacco from his shirt pocket, took a pinch, and loaded his bottom lip. "If you're ever in a situation where you have to pull a gun on someone, you need to shoot to kill. Chances are he'll be bigger than you; and he'll be liable to get the gun, and you'll be the one dead. Understand?"

"Yeah."

"Never ever pull a gun unless you're willing to see it through." He put the tin of tobacco in his shirt pocket filled with pens and screwdrivers and his notebook. "Got it?"

"Got it."

He smiled and clapped me on the back. "All right, pard. All right."

He also bought new camping gear. Mummy bags and backpacks and had my mother cut up old clothing to make stuff sacks for survival gear. He bought me a survival kit that came with road flares, a coiled tree saw, instant-shelter, poncho, water purifying tablets, and on and on. Again, it was a "just in case" gesture. Man to man. Father to son. *Here is what you need to survive this world when things get ugly.* Some of the conversations between my grandfather and dad involved building underground homes with roof-top gardens. "We could build them on the ranch," my grandfather reasoned. The homes would be efficient and, most important, out of sight.

Soon, Dad found work in the southeastern desert of Utah, not too far from Roosevelt, where he had grown up. He would be working in a man-camp, a rough-and-tumble operation rife with drifters and drunks, a place whose population was not entirely unlike those who boarded at the Enders Hotel. The camp comprised a cluster of dust-blown, tar-paper trailers and tents and Dad would drive the 690 miles round trip every weekend to come back to the Enders to run payroll, to cut meat, and attend to the current repairs that demanded his attention. In his absence, I was to take on a larger share of the workload, a notion I resisted at once.

Nevertheless, when Dad's green truck idled out of the Enders parking lot I couldn't help but wonder whether or not he would return.

185

31. A Common Story

As the warm weather arrived, B.J. and I kicked around town more often, ducking behind buildings to smoke our smokes. Things were hard at his house too. His father was unemployed and his car seemed forever moored in front of the bars. And while his father knocked back his afternoon beers in Stockman's Tavern, his mother was across the street in Laura's, the competing bar, mooning over her own drinks. When B.J. needed money, we sent word into one tavern or the other, loitering in its darkening doorway, and sooner or later, one of his parents would emerge with a few bills, and advice to stay the hell out of trouble. Some days we waited longer than others and once I remember glancing at a station wagon parked in front of the bar loaded with four scraggly kids—three of whom appeared to be playing tag over the seats, while one, a girl, stared emptily at us standing in the doorway. I waved and offered a smile, but she stared right through me. I knew that story. The kids waiting for their parents in the bar. That was a common story.

32. Bear

Shortly after Dad took the job in Roosevelt, a guy who insisted we call him *Bear* moved into Number 3, the apartment where Trapper Jim had stayed. He fancied himself a modern day mountain man who owned a truck with a camper shell whose license plate read BEAR. He also owned a Honda Goldwing motorcycle with an upright grizzly airbrushed on the gas tank. He wouldn't stay long, a month or so, but I'll never forget him. The first day I saw him he was washing his motorcycle with our long green hose. He was bearded and fat and wore a necklace of bear claws and a leather vest with no shirt underneath so his enormous hairy belly hung down over his jeans. He called me over. "Hey, you see this bike?"

"Yeah. It's nice," I said squinting in the sun.

"You're goddamn right it is. And you're gonna stay the hell away from it. Savvy?"

I took a step backward as if I had been slugged. "Yeah. Sure. *Whatever*," I said and walked away.

No one liked Bear especially the handful of haggard women I watched storm from Number 3 smoothing their clothes muttering, "*Sonofabitch*."

33. Other Places

In all the years I spent around the railroad tracks near the Enders Hotel, I saw a passenger train very rarely. But when one huffed into town, everything in my world stopped. To see a train like that was extraordinary—even in my chip-on-the-shoulder teenage years. Its mere presence was magical somehow. It was like time had suddenly hurled me back to a more glamorous era when women wore white gloves and waved from those windows, and when golden boys wore crisp slacks and polished loafers off to war. Trains like that, I imagined, had arrived from somewhere important, more significant, as if from a dream. And trains like that, I knew, were bound for other places beyond the sagebrush valley of Soda Springs, Idaho. They were traveling to places that mattered. So when one pulled into town on a summer afternoon and slowed to a stop with its brakes hissing, I took notice. I had been outside near the clubhouse I had nearly outgrown. When the train stopped, I kicked through the wet grass, hit the parking lot, and sprinted the two hundred yards toward the tracks as if I might be in danger of missing something, as if my father might step off with his suitcases. My chest heaved as I sucked rain-spent air, and a trickle of sweat slid down my side. I wiped my forehead as I picked up the pace. I waved to the faces peering out the windows of the train, searching them for familiarity.

I stopped near the tracks and stood close enough that I could feel the train's heat on my face. And there in its elongated shadow, I considered briefly—as I often did when near a train—stowing away. I knew that if I ever had to run away for good, I would hop a train. I never settled on a direction, though. A westbound train would whisk me into Pocatello and then California, perhaps. I imagined the rails ending abruptly at the ocean, waves clapping over the iron rails. But if I had jumped an eastbound train, I would rumble toward Wyoming. But I couldn't imagine anything beyond that windy, rock-torn state. What was after Wyoming, I wondered? Chicago? Detroit? New York, certainly. Cities I had never heard of. Moments later, the train lurched forward. One or two people gave me a courtesy wave, and the train pulled west.

34. Trouble

With Dad working in the man-camp in Utah, and my mother and grandmother swamped in work, my days and nights became freer. B.J. and I spent almost every night at Double Kwik, smoking cigarettes, playing videogames, and bullshitting with Robert, the cashier. More than once we hung around with empty pockets hoping to find spare change in the return slots of the videogames in the back. One particular night, though, our curiosity led us beyond Double Kwik and into the Laundromat next door. "I'll guarantee we'll find some change there," B.J. said. And so I followed.

The Laundromat was well lit with buzzing fluorescent lights and empty. We checked the change returns on the candy and soda and fabric softener machines. Looked for loose change behind a row of washers. Checked the change return on the pay phone. But found nothing. Then one of us (I forget which) started fiddling with the cashbox on one of the dryers. Its small door wiggled back and forth and seemed like it could be jimmied easily.

This is how one thing leads to another.

At some point, a guy B.J. knew through his older brother, David, pulled into the Laundromat parking lot in his beige and rusted-out Plymouth Duster. His name was Mario and he was eighteen. And it was Mario who gave us the tire iron.

It felt good to take the tire iron to that first coin-op washing machine, and to strike a solid blow to its coin box. B.J. stood by and laughed. "Fuck, man," he said. "Let me see that son-of-a bitch." He took the iron and hit the cream-colored face of the machine over and over again until he was winded. Then I grabbed it and smashed another box open. Our eyes dazzled at the sight of all those quarters spilling out.

Then we moved to the next machine. We smashed that tire iron against metal, metal against metal against metal, and beat those coin boxes until every cherry popped and we got exactly what we wanted. One machine down, then another, and another. We filled our pockets with quarters. The rest we kicked across the floor. And when we finished smashing the coin boxes we started kicking tables and the chairs and the dryers. And we stood there in that brightly lit room of wreckage dripping with sweat, our chests heaving, and feeling, perhaps, like we had finally gotten even.

On our way out I took the tire iron to the pay phone. B.J. hesitated with a chuckle that was tempered with seriousness. "Come on man. Let's get the fuck out of here." But I didn't hear him. I grabbed that iron and took a running swing right at that phone. The gray plastic receiver exploded on the first strike. I swung and swung and swung. The face of the phone began to cave. I went for the coin box. Over and over again, I threw my entire body into my swings, stopping only to clear a strand of hair from my eyes. I had never felt so resolved in all my life.

Later, Mario returned and took what must have been a bucket of quarters, and bought over a case of beer from Robert at the Double Kwik (Robert would sell us smokes but stopped short of selling us beer, and Mario had a fake ID). We loaded up in his Duster and drove under the overpass and guzzled several beers at the edge of the railroad tracks. B.J. sat and smoked a cigarette while I drained another beer and hucked rocks into the night. Mario kept shaking his head. "You guys are some crazy motherfuckers."

We laughed.

"I mean you really fucked that place up."

"Fuck it," B.J. said and exhaled a drag.

I belched and flicked an empty beer can into the weeds by the tracks. I looked down the tracks to the east, turned and stared toward the west. The sky was orange: Monsanto. It was late. And I needed to go home. "I've got to split," I said and started down the tracks toward the hotel.

"You need a ride, man?" Mario asked.

"Naw, thanks though."

"Yeah. I'd better head, too," B.J. said and stood.

"But the night is *young*," Mario tried.

"I think I'll walk, too," B.J. said.

"You sure?"

B.J. looked down the tracks and said, "Hey, B.S."

I stopped and looked back.

"I'll see you around."

"Yeah," I said.

The next morning I woke and my body was wracked from the night's exertion. Plus I felt sick. I could hardly move. I was in deep trouble of course. For coming in that late and the arguments and fights ensued.

Two days later, the cops had caught up with us. We had an at-home wrestling tournament and a few minutes before I strapped my headgear on and stepped on to the mat, I saw two police officers enter the junior high gymnasium. One of the cops I knew well because his wife, Becky, worked for us at the café. The two police officers chatted casually with several people in the stands and stood at the edge of the mat with their arms folded in front of them like everything was normal. I felt nauseous. My knees were shot of their strength and I thought I might collapse. I knew they were there for me—for us. The referee drew my opponent and me out onto the dark-blue mat. My knees quivered. My eyes blurred. I felt like all the muscles in my body had gone loose. I couldn't focus. When the ref said *wrestle* and chopped his hand between us, my opponent lunged. I saw the ceiling of our gymnasium and all of its bright lights. I saw the catwalk and heating ducts. My face burned red and a tear leaked out of the corner of my eye. In moments the ref slapped his hand to the mat and it was over. I had lost. The two police officers, who had already nabbed B.J., escorted me off the mat and Hinajosa—our squat, balding coach—threw me a look of contempt and shook his head. The cheerleaders ducked their heads behind their blue and gold pom-poms to mask their birdsong. My teammates stared on slack-jawed as we disappeared under the stands and into the locker room. The crowd, that sea of indistinct faces, pivoted in the bleachers and followed the spectacle. Many of them, no doubt, would have known me from the café.

In the following weeks, we appeared separately before a juvenile court that meted out our sentences. It is difficult to define the parameters of status in a small agrarian town, but it seems that I had more than B.J. I don't recall his exact punishment, but I know it was far worse than mine. David had been in trouble with cops a number of times and in the overall scheme of small-town jurisprudence, familial associations were not just seen as precedents, preemptive indictments, but as literal indications of what the future held in store. As an only child I had no such precedent. And I had the added advantage of knowing the cops. I was the kid who lived in the Enders Hotel. After all, two of our waitresses were married to police officers.

My restitution was laughable. I had to wash and wax *all* the Soda Springs police vehicles including two ambulances and two fire engines. I washed a total of *one* squad car before one of the officers, a tall broad man with thin grayish hair, came out and asked if I thought I had learned my lesson. I said I had learned my lesson, absolutely. He looked into a blank spot of sky, hitched up his brown pants, and said, "Then go on, and get out of here."

35. The Cowboy

The job in Roosevelt drew to a close as all jobs do, and Dad returned to the dailiness of the Enders. I had been grounded for
my "little stunt" at the Laundromat. *Little stunt*, that's what my
grandmother called it. "Your grandfather wouldn't be too proud
of you," she said and I hung my head.

I was in the café at the yellow counter eating some lunch when
my mother took a stool, drew a cigarette to her mouth, lit it, and
pulled an ashtray near. "You'll never guess who I just got off the
phone with," she said, exhaling. She was excited and upbeat, despite being physically and visibly tired, despite my recent trouble.
I could always tell when her energy dropped or slackened. Tired-
ness was as much an extension of grief in those emotionally taut
days as it was the result of work consuming the hours, and the days
and nights bleeding together into a constant smudge one had to
endure. When she was tired, she always removed her glasses and
rubbed her eyes. Her slight amblyopic gaze betrayed her exhaus-
tion, as her left eye wandered slightly from center.

"Who?"

"Your Grandpa George."

The name registered. George Moyer—my mother's biological father. I grabbed my cheeseburger with both hands. "Oh, yeah?"

"He'll be here early next week. He's just *dying* to see you."

"Cool." The last time I saw him I was two and had no recollection of him at all. Like my biological father, George Moyer was just as distant, abstract, and ghostly. I had always wanted to know what parts of George looked like me and it was difficult to tell from the one or two pictures I had seen of him. And of course, I had never seen a picture of my father and so that was a complete blank. Sometimes I would crawl out of bed to stand before the mirror in the bathroom in my underwear and stare at the image of myself staring back. I would subtract the immediately recognizable features: my eyes, cheekbones, chin, those that came from my mother. Then I would isolate the unfamiliar contours of the face in the mirror—the forehead, eyebrows, lips(?), nose(?), and assign them to one of the invisible men who preceded me as if it were a puzzle to be solved. But the thought of seeing my biological grandfather in a matter of days quickened my pulse.

"How long will he be here?"

"A while I would imagine."

"What's he like? Like what's he *really* like?" I asked as I drew a fry through a puddle of ketchup.

"You'd like him. He's funny. *God*, he's funny." My mother took a deep drag and let it go and it looked as thick as cream above the counter. "He's all cowboy, and just has the *best* sense of humor. He's great. You two will get along so well. I can't wait."

"Is Grandma, you know, like, *okay* about this? Like won't that be weird or something?"

"I don't see why it should be. They're adults and all that shit between them happened so long ago that it don't matter anyway." She gave a wave of her hand as if batting away the past.

I nodded and took a bite from my cheeseburger. She stubbed out her cigarette and slid the ashtray toward the end of the counter and stood. "Well, I got to get back to it." And she slipped into the back of the kitchen and into the constant thrum of business.

That next week, as promised, a blue Ford pickup with a camper shell appeared in front of the Enders Hotel, and two men stepped out, stretched, and entered the café. I had been taking a soda break between chores and decided to stick around at my mother's behest. George would be arriving soon. When they stepped into the café, customers gave them a casual appraisal, and my mother greeted them with open arms. "Brandon," she called to me. "Come here. This is your grandpa and," she said turning to the other guy who was maybe ten years older than me, "your uncle Larry."

I waved and was immediately comforted that Larry also had long hair, an earring, and, perhaps best of all, a Mötley Crüe T-shirt. We shook hands all around and George was just what I thought he would be. Leathery, cowboyish, bowlegged, box-jawed and barrel-chested. He wore glasses and had a gentleness that seemed to belie his rugged stature. I also noticed he wore hearing aids and a leather belt with GEORGE stamped into its hide and dyed red. He had my cheekbones and nose and ears. Larry, who was born to George's second wife, Eunice—a woman I only knew by name, and whose name stuck out in my mind because it was *Eunice*—looked only vaguely familiar. Something about the setting of his eyes, the sunken bridge of his nose, his prominent cheekbones said that he, too, had one foot in this bloodline.

We sat down at a table and Janet brought cups of coffee and waters and refilled my soda and brought Larry one, too. "You like Mötley Crüe?" I asked.

"Yeah. Caught them a couple of years ago in Seattle. Good show. You like them?"

I told him I did, which was true, although his shirt came from the *Theatre of Pain* tour, and I wasn't a particular fan of that album partly because it was so popular and partly because it seemed overly *glam*, a term B.J., Sherrod, and I used often with evident amounts of derision. ("They look like *chicks*," we'd say of the band members.) Then I conceded I liked their older stuff more.

Larry nodded quickly as if I had beat him to the observation he was going to make. "Oh, me, too. Me, too."

Inevitably, a lull grew in the conversation, and I drained my soda through the clear straw and my mother lit another cigarette.

"So, Brandon," George said. "What subjects you taking in school?"

"Like what do I like?"

He nodded and fiddled with his shirt pocket.

"I like English, I guess. Books and stuff. And science. But I *hate* math."

He laughed. "I fought math, too. And math won. But I remember liking literature. Course I didn't make it that far before I decided to go cowboyin'. Guess I'd read too many westerns. Put some ideas in my head."

Everyone laughed.

Just then my grandmother stepped out from the kitchen and approached our table, but it was clear that she wasn't going to take a seat.

"Sit, Mom," my mother said.

"If I sit, I'll never get back up," she said and laughed.

"I see some things never change," George said. "She was *always* going," he said looking right at me as if it was a secret between the two of us.

"You look good," my grandmother said.

"So do you. You remember Larry?"

"It's been years."

"Hi, Beth," Larry said. "Sorry to hear about Lynn."

George tapped the sides of his coffee cup. "Yeah, sorry to hear about that. He was a helluva man. Through and through. Really was."

"Well, these things happen. But there's one thing about it: at least he's not suffering anymore. So thank God for that."

We each nodded the way you do when you hear such affirmative statements.

Mom asked my grandmother a business-related question which changed the tack and tone of the conversation and released my grandmother and all of us from this strained if not awkward situation.

"Well," my grandmother said addressing George. "Karen's got your room key and you should have everything you need. If not, shout. Good seeing you."

"Thanks. You, too."

She stepped into the lobby and disappeared toward the apartment.

Larry stayed only a week before he moved on. George drove him to Salt Lake City where he caught a plane to Oregon to visit his brother Lance, another half-uncle I had not met. But in that week I got to know him well. Also in that time, my cousin Vince had once again moved back into the Enders Hotel with his mom, so the three of us started spending time together. On one of the first nights together, Larry said, "I've got something for you guys." He slipped out the back apartment door into the rear parking lot and returned with two five-foot lengths of black pipe with the diameter of a magic marker. "Blow-guns," he said. "Picked these up in Rock Springs and thought of you guys. Check them out."

He pulled out a baggie of yellow darts crafted from 20-guage shotgun waddings and Sheetrock nails.

"Cool," we said in unison.

I loaded a plastic yellow dart into the blowing end of the pipe, aimed the blow-gun at the floor, and blew. The dart stuck easily into the floor. Vince shot his at a shoebox I had pulled from a closet and had set on the floor of my bedroom. Larry followed suit and shot his into the shoebox as well. This went on for more than an hour and then, as if planned in advance, Vince looked at Larry and said, "You ready?"

Larry looked at his watch and said, "Yeah." Then he looked at me smiling. "Don't fill this place full of holes, dude."

"Where you guys going?"

"Just around," Vince said.

I could tell that I was not invited.

Only later would I get it out of Vince that they had gone to split a six-pack, and Larry didn't think I should go on account of my age, a fact I resented deeply. "Chill," Vince had said. "He was just looking out for you. That's all."

The most surprising thing about George's visit was that it wasn't, nor had it ever been intended to be short-term. But I didn't get a sense of this even when I asked again how long he was staying. "Awhile," was all I heard.

And so like any other guest, he stayed in a room upstairs. Eventually my grandmother put her ex-husband to work around the hotel where I would occasionally run into him in a hallway sanding doorjambs, or see him on a ladder replacing a bulb. It gave me the strangest feeling. It was as if he was just another drifter, another ender who had turned to us because there was no other place or person he could turn to. And while I did not know it at the time, there was some truth in that feeling. George did not have a home per se. He had lived in a trailer in Sheridan, Wyoming, after he and Eunice split. And he lived in a trailer in Benson, Arizona, where his sister—my great aunt Vie, a woman I knew and admired deeply for her generosity and for the staggering amount of turquoise she wore—kept a winter trailer. But other than that George roamed in his truck and slept in its shell. He seemed to have occupied a temporary world.

His presence also gave me a strange feeling because it was as if he was trying to take the place of Lynn Beus, my real grandfather. This feeling crystallized one afternoon when I saw him in the basement in the Tool Room fetching a few things for whatever project he was working on. The hammer he held, one I recognized because I had used it many times, had etched on the side of its weighty head, LYNN B, the same inscription all our tools bore. I looked at George's hand wrapped around the wooden handle of the hammer—its grains worn smooth by my grandfather's hands—and I felt cross-wired in the moment. While I looked for faint resemblances in his hands, traits that I might have had in my own hands, I also felt like those etched letters LYNN B filled the room somehow, that they could conjure his ghost, and there was no way that I could look away from them and the strangeness of George's hands so near to them, and I remember talking but not listening, just looking and nodding, as if we were underwater or in a dream, caught between worlds.

A few days later, I knocked on my mother's apartment door. She was in her tiny kitchen making a batch of cookies for George. "What's happening?" she asked.

"Not much."

"What's on the agenda today?"

I shrugged and grabbed a cookie. "Looks like George—er, Grandpa will be here for awhile then?"

"I guess so," she said. "Looks like he got that job."

"What job?"

"Forest Service. Didn't I tell you?"

"No," I said and took a bite. The cookie was still soft from her oven that was so small it appeared toy-like. "That's weird."

"What?"

"So he's like *living* here?"

"Yeah. What's weird about that? I think it's great."

"Oh, it is great. But weird, too. You know."

"Weird how?"

"With Grandma and all," I said and looked out the window into the parking lot. The geyser was going off and a gaggle of tourists stood around snapping pictures of it. "I mean, you don't think they'll get back together?"

"*Mom and Dad*? Are you kidding me? Oh, no. Not in a million years."

"Then why is he here? Now?"

"To spend time with me and you and Buddy. But mostly me and you."

"Huh," I said.

"He's not getting any younger, Brandon, and the man has to be thinking that the day will come when it might be too late to spend some time with his family."

I nodded, thinking it over. It made sense. It made too much sense.

"Speaking of which," she said, opening the oven door. "He wants to get out and see some of the country around here tomorrow, and asked if you would want to go with him."

"And do what?"

"I don't know. Just go on a drive."

"That's it?"

"I know he has a gun—cowboy that he is—and wants to do some target practice. You could do that."

"And you'd be okay with that?"

"You know as well as I do that I am outvoted on the gun issue around here. Besides, as long as you get to spend some time with him, I don't care what you do."

"All right." I grabbed another cookie for the road and said goodbye.

The next day had already been arranged. My mother woke me at seven o'clock to tell me that George was waiting for me in the café for breakfast. I rolled out of bed, rubbed my eyes, dressed, and went over to join him.

The café was alive with voices and laughter, and I spotted George sitting at a table reading a paper with coffee. I took a seat and ordered a coffee too.

"Morning," he said shuffling the paper.

"Morning." I yawned and looked around. The place was sunlit. "You eat yet?"

"Not yet. Thought I'd wait for you."

Shortly, we ordered breakfast and talked casually about the first subjects to arise: He loved to fish and hunt but mostly fish. I told him I had hunted before but not much and fished some, trying to sound enthusiastic about engaging either sport in the near future. The truth was that I didn't really care if I hunted or fished again despite the rural code that said in order to be a man I ought to hunt and fish, and that if I didn't something was wrong with me. This nagging I tried to beat back, though, and it helped to have friends like B.J., Nick, and Sherrod who didn't hunt or fish either.

He looked around and said, "I bet it's nice living here."

I shrugged, and as Tootie brought a coffee thermos to refill George's cup, he added, with a wink, "And to have all these pretty waitresses bringing you food." Tootie cackled and waved him off. "Must be something."

"It's all right, I guess. But I got plenty to do around here," I added mitigating the perceived life of ease with a dose of work ethic so that he wouldn't think less of me for my circumstance.

"When I was a pup over there to Jackson we lived in a tent for awhile." He chuckled and buttered his toast. "Then Mom built a one-room cabin for us. We thought that was the stuff. To have a roof and a floor and a window."

"Wow. Must have been hard."

"We didn't know anything else. Besides we lived in Jackson. Doesn't get much better than that. To have the Tetons as your backyard. I guess a guy could do worse."

I nodded and took a strip of bacon.

I had heard stories of the tent they lived in and would years later see a photograph. An old battered black-and-white creased down the center. George sits in a patch of tallgrass. He is all of two years old. He looks like the infant version of myself. The canvas tent is to his right, its flap drawn back. It looks like a tiny boat tossed in a sea of brush. The Tetons rise in the background.

Only years later would I get the rest of the story, the series of events that would lead my great-grandmother to live in a tent with four children. Only then would I learn that her husband, Fred Moyer, a swaggering cowboy himself, had one eye trained on the hope of a new rainbow, and had given his life over to the futility of chasing rather than surrender to rootedness. Only years later would I see a photograph of this elusive man. The photograph, though, was snapped under a noon sun and his black cowboy hat threw a shadow over his face so dark it seemed to swallow him whole. It was a photograph befitting of his legacy. Inevitably his rainbows called him farther away while debts accrued in Jackson and his wife, my great-grandmother, gathered her four young children, and made the decision that they were better off in a tent on the rolling brush plain than to stay tethered to a drifter who seemed fated to cast his last nickel to the wind.

The story is not new of course. And perhaps what pained me so much years later was that it was so common, indeed too common. I would learn, too, that my great-grandmother was no stranger to that kind of lifestyle. Her parents had tramped around the west for twenty-six years and had thirteen children, no two born in the same place, along the way. Bessie, my great-grandmother, was literally born in the back of a wagon on Teton pass in July 1902.

The generations move with a force all their own, and the patterns seem to oblige. It seems fitting, inevitable perhaps, that we eventually bought a hotel, a place outfitted with so many exits and entrances, and a place that seemed itself a beacon to the far-farers, to people, ultimately, like us.

After we cleaned our plates, we set out into the bright summer light, climbed into George's blue Ford pickup and set out for roads unknown. "Where do you want to go?" he asked.

"I don't care. What do you want to see?"

George pulled a Forest Service map from the glove compartment, unfolded it, and adjusted his glasses. "I guess I'll be working over here," he said pointing to a patch of green southeast of Soda Springs.

I studied the map and recognized the names. "That's Eight Mile. It's like a canyon—I think. Yeah. You want to go there?"

"Is there much to see? I can't remember if I've been there or not. It's been so long."

"It's pretty cool," I said meaning both *pretty* and *cool* but not wanting either term to stand alone. Pretty might not settle with this cowboy. And cool seemed, well, too boyish.

"Let's go there, then." George scratched his chin and refolded the well-used map. When he had drawn his chin up, I saw a scar on his throat the size of a penny.

"What happened to your neck?"

He laughed. "Gun shot."

"You got shot?"

"In the war."

"Whoa. What happened?"

George started the pickup, ground the stick-shifter into reverse, and idled us out of the parking lot. The sun blazed on the truck hood and I rolled my window down.

"We were in Guam. Infantry, you know. And I was on an early morning patrol on a hillside. And that's when it happened. Felt like a freight train had knocked me to the ground. All I saw was the sky."

"The bullet went in your neck? Where did it come out?"

"Actually it came *out* my neck. But it entered below my ear, here," he said and pointed behind his lobe. "Then it ricocheted off a tooth, and came out here."

"*Whoa.*" I was completely taken with the story. "Did it hurt?"

"Not at first. I didn't even know I had been shot. I knew I had been knocked down but that was it. But then my mouth was filled with blood and I thought I was dead. My patrol thought I was dead. Head shot, you know. And there I was trying to tell them I was alive while gargling blood."

George was filled with such stories. Stories of becoming a bucka-roo in Wyoming before the war. Stories of traveling around the coun-

204

try. "The only time I was ever in New York, my truck and camper caught fire," he said as we drove along a canyon road. "But I didn't know it was on fire until all these people passing me kept waving frantically and pointing and yelling *fire*! Then I got the message." He paused as if conjuring the next lines of the story. "So I get the outfit pulled over and jump out and there's nothing I can do. So some guy stops to help and we just stand there watching the whole thing go up. Pretty soon we can hear small explosions and things were shooting into the air like rockets. And this guy, he says, 'What do you suppose that was?' And I says, 'I think it was a can of beans.'"

He laughed. And I laughed too. I thought that was a good one. The consummate storyteller. He told stories about traveling to Area 51, about trying to sneak in and get a peak, but being driven out at the last minute. He told stories about bear encounters and how once he thought he had seen Bigfoot.

"You believe in Bigfoot?" I asked as we bumped along a set of meadow ruts.

He looked out the window. "All I can say for sure is that critics always say if there was such a thing, we would have found its bones. But think about this. How often have you seen a bear skeleton?" He looked at me.

"Never."

"Me either. And I've spent most of my life in the mountains, in bear country, and I have yet to see so much as a trace of bear bones. But that's just one way of looking at it. Is there such a thing? I don't know. But anything is possible, I suppose."

At noon we stopped along a draw near a stream and got out and stretched. We had packed bacon, lettuce, and tomato sandwiches, cold pop, and chips. I pulled out my lunch while George shuffled over to the creek, crouched, and dipped his hand, pulling up a handful of smooth stones. "A guy might try panning for gold up here. Might be surprised at what you find."

"You ever find gold?"

"Not enough to take to the bank, but I've found some."

George opened his camper shell door and dropped the tailgate so we could sit and eat our lunch. "When I was about your age, I remember thinking it would be all right to live forever out in a place like this."

I looked around the meadow and the stream that ran through and the ponderosa that fringed the meadow and imagined what that must be like, and how part of me would like that, too. "One of my favorite shows used to be *Grizzly Adams*," I said. "He lived in a place like this," I said motioning to the meadow.

"I seem to remember that program. Earthy fella, Mr. Adams. But I think he had the right idea. I always liked that *Gunsmoke*. You ever watch that one?"

"Sometimes."

"That was a good one. Used to watch *The Virginian*, too. Read the book, too. You read that in school?"

"I don't think so. But we read *Shane*."

"Now *there's* a good one. You like it?"

"Oh, yeah. I liked that one a lot," I said.

"Books like that seem few and far between nowadays. I think they stopped writing the classics in the fifties."

"Probably," I said missing the wryness of his joke. I took a generous bite of my sandwich which was very good, and the bacon was crisp and just right. "Ever heard of *The Outsiders*?" I asked with a mouthful of sandwich.

"Can't say that I have."

"That's a good book."

"I'll have to look it up at the library."

After lunch George pulled out a black .44 from behind his truck seat and a box of cartridges. "You ever shoot one of these?"

I shook my head. "Shot lots of rifles. Mom don't like pistols."

He nodded and looked out across the meadow. "We got to find us a target."

I spotted a green beer bottle peeking out from a sagebrush across the stream, and made a sprint for it. It was propped against an anthill so I grabbed it quickly and high-stepped away from the hill. "How about this?"

"Good. Set it on that fencepost yonder there."

When I crossed back to the truck, George handed me the loaded pistol. I was surprised by its heft, but even more surprised when I fired the first round by the kick and near unbearable ring that stabbed through my ears. A cloud of dirt shot up about five feet beyond the green bottle and I was embarrassed by the shot.

"Steady it up," George said. "Put the bead on the green. Squeeze when you're ready."

It took me three rounds before I shattered the bottle, but when I did I could tell that George was pleased and not embarrassed and for this I was unendingly happy.

By afternoon's end the bullets had been spent and our pop was gone and the empty cans were punctured and torn with gunfire. It was hot and sweat glistened on our foreheads, so we decided to call it a day, and headed back to the hotel.

A week or so later, I asked my grandmother about George staying in the hotel and if she found it strange. She was in the apartment taking a break in her recliner with a book. Her feet were up, and Ribbons lay in her lap dozing. She looked up and gave a trimmed, quick, and calculated response: "Lots of people stay here and help us out. Why is he any different?"

Her question was rhetorical, and the conversation was over.

That summer looked and felt like any other summer with the single exception of George staying as our guest. I listened to Rock 103 while I cut meat in the walk-in, or hung Sheetrock upstairs in the hotel. And I painted eves over apartment entrances and occasionally, on weekends, I would see George shampooing carpets or oiling a squeaking door hinge.

And then one day, he left. His job with the Forest Service had drawn to a close and he loaded his camper shell and said goodbye. I had watched his truck leave the parking lot as I had watched so many men before him vanish, and I felt emptier inside than I had in a very long time.

36. B.J.

There was no falling out as there often is between friends of our particular bond. There was no fight, no fuck you, nothing. It was like he was there all my life, and then one day, he was gone. His parents, who had been drinking recklessly in separate bars, divorced, and B.J. moved with his mother an hour and a half south to Logan, Utah, where my grandfather had died.

Because they had no money and because B.J. had a little brother and sister to look after, he dropped out of high school and went to work. And when he wasn't working, he was doing crank and staying out all night and getting into trouble. David was doing some stints in jail for drugs and showed up only occasionally to borrow money. I learned about this unraveling in the terrible, clumsy way people learn about others in small towns—through hallway gossip. Friends of friends. I didn't know what to believe and what not to believe. Did you hear B.J. has been doing PCP, angel dust, coke? These stories seemed incredible, impossible. But part of me could also believe them.

Eventually, I stopped hearing even the rumors. He had vanished.

In those first years of high school I became obsessed with playing the guitar and wooing girls in equal amounts. I practiced every night, loudly. Usually too loudly. Once, when Dad was in one of his better moods, he stepped into my room and asked if I could turn it down a notch as my bedroom shared a wall with the café's dining room. "Until you sound as good as Chuck Berry, let's keep it at a dull roar, huh?"

I laughed and turned it down. Then I spent the next weeks learning Chuck Berry songs just to show him that I could.

Music became the thing. Sherrod and I were serious about music. Before long, Sherrod had joined a band and I was invited to jam, but not invited back because I wasn't yet good enough. Rejection was all I needed. Three-hour practice sessions turned into five, and five turned into seven. Homework went undone or only partially done. Playing guitar was the only thing that mattered. Before the year was out, I was asked to join the band. I couldn't have been happier.

About a year and half after B.J. disappeared, I received a thick letter from him in the mail. The letter was covered with metal bands' insignias: KISS, OZZY, SCORPIONS, and the like. That wasn't strange. It was classic B.J. What was strange was the return address. It was some kind of hospital.

He had been checked into a drug rehab.

The rumors, as it turns out, were true. He had dropped out of high school. He did have to support his family including his mother and father. He was an addict, but there was one other thing, that I hadn't heard: he had met a girl and had gotten her pregnant. The girl already had a four-year-old boy. He was going to marry her once he "got clean."

I wrote back giving him some encouraging words. After that, the letters came regularly. One a week. Most detailed rehab life. "You wouldn't believe all the fucked-up people in this hell-hole," he wrote. "I can't wait to get on with the rest of my life." The days, he said, dragged on. "I can't even have a smoke because I'm under age. And you know me and my niccy-fits." But he also wrote about growing up, about when we were younger. About the clubhouse and about Soda Creek. "You remember that goddamn raft we tried to build?"

And I would write back talking about the band and jamming and about girls. About how I had started taking girls into empty rooms upstairs and undressing them on clean beds, and how if the Enders Hotel was good for anything, it was good for getting laid.

The letters got longer and longer. More detailed. And more and more they talked about how much he hated Soda Springs. "That town could fucking get nuked and I wouldn't give a flying shit. I fucking hate that place. All my life those people said I wouldn't turn out to be nothing, but when I get out of here, I am going to prove those fuckers wrong if it's the last thing I do."

And I believed him.

Eventually, though, the letters trickled off, and B.J. became a mystery. Just another guy who was out there somewhere.

37. After Labor Day

Not long after B.J.'s letters stopped arriving in our post office box, my grandmother made a decision that in hindsight would seem fated but at the time seemed, at least to me, unthinkable, treasonous.

On a sluggish afternoon some two weeks before Labor Day, my grandmother found herself in the kitchen preparing a Daily Specials menu for the coming week. Business was slow and had been for some time. We were enduring the bust end of mining-town cycle. And she was deeply tired. Tired in her bones. She looked around, wiped a bead of sweat from her forehead, and scanned the list of supplies she would have to order for the coming week. That is when she put the pen down and called the cook, dishwasher, and two waitresses together for a meeting.

"We'll close for Labor Day," she said. "And that will be it. I'm done."

They were stunned. The one waitress, Tootie, started to cry for what could only have been practical reasons: jobs in Soda Springs were few and far between and she had worked at the Enders for ten years.

My grandmother simply couldn't do it anymore. The sign in the window would be permanently turned from OPEN to CLOSED. I saw her decision as treasonous because, ultimately, I wanted it both ways. I wanted out of the Enders. But that didn't mean I wanted *it* gone. It was my home.

So there the café and hotel sat. Empty, abandoned, ghosted. Chairs stacked on tables. Lights out. Boxes stacked on the counter. Done. It was the most depressing sight I had ever seen. The only thing that remained open, that indeed remained lucrative, was the bar, which was leased out. Always in Soda Springs, boom or bust, the bars survive. "When the churches and bars close down, then you'll know this town has sunk," my grandmother was fond of saying.

So the weeks tumbled by, one stacking on another, and invariably I would watch a hapless soul step to the café door and give it a tug not having seen the sign. But it was locked. Confused, the person would peer in the window for any sign of life, shrug, and walk away. But eventually even this pattern would fade as the reality slowly set in. The Enders Hotel and Café was closed.

Six months passed and the café and hotel sat empty. In that time, I had thrown myself headlong into music. Sherrod and I were in a band and we played different gigs around the county. Birthday parties, high school dances, pep assemblies, and the like. We were fiercely competitive. In school. With girls. In music. Everything. Inevitably, gradually, our interests parted and even our competitive spirits waned as our futures seemed plotted in different directions. As a result we spent less and less time hanging out and jamming, and the band dissolved. Sherrod became another passing face in the hallway. And I started hanging out with a group of Mormon kids, slick-haired smiling youths with nice clothes, clean mouths, and who seemed thrilled that I had crossed over into their confidence. I had even gone so far as to get baptized into the Mormon religion (even though I secretly thought it hokey and dubious at best). Following my baptism, my popularity soared almost overnight. I was voted class favorite and was elected Student Body Vice President (no large feat, really, in a small, close-knit rural Idaho school). I joined clubs and service organizations. I acted in plays. I sang in choir. I started reading more and more books, and began writing very bad poetry. Girls paid attention to me. Everyone I knew was talking about college. This was a foreign world, a new world, and I could not have walked taller, could not have been happier.

38. New Management

When my grandmother got a phone call from Rose, one of her former cooks, offering to take over the café with her husband Frank Sr.—a wiry man with bulging eyes, a crew cut, and a roaring temper—my grandmother leapt. "We can do this," Rose said.

They had big plans. They would change the name, which to my grandmother's thinking, was the wrong move. But she said nothing to them. They were going to turn that place around. Soda Springs wouldn't know what hit them. My mother agreed to go to work for them. So did many from the original crew.

Six more months passed and my grandmother got another phone call from Rose. *We can't do it anymore,* she had said. *We had no idea. The expenses. My God, the expenses. And the time. We're sorry.*

When my grandmother broke the news to my mother and dad, they resisted. Or at least my mother did. "I'll do it," she had said.

"You'll do what?"

"I'll run it."

"Like hell you will."

"We'll lease it from you and we will manage it."

Why, exactly, Dad agreed to such an encumbering commitment when the situation would have otherwise set him free remains a mystery. The news made a small blip in the local paper: *Karen Schrand to take over Enders.*

The Enders Café was restored from whatever Frank and Rose had named it—a name that is now utterly forgotten. And my mother and dad went to work. My grandmother worked as a dinner cook and helped open in the mornings. The roles had been reversed.

Everything seemed the same with one exception, a stern one that my mother insisted on. "We won't live here," she said. "If we're going to make this work and maintain any kind of sense of a family, we will not live under the same roof we work under." So my mother and dad bought the house my grandmother had grown up in, one that had been in the family ever since. We called it the Gray House. It was an ugly thing. Two stories. Tall and narrow like a giant milk carton, it stood on the main drag. During World War I, it had been a train station on the eastern edge of town. Then shortly before World War II, my great-grandfather bought it and had it moved into town on sleds drawn by a team of horses. He covered it with gray asphalt shingling which earned it its name. But by the time my mother and dad bought it from my grandmother, its windows had been blown out and were covered by boards or garbage sacks or plastic sheeting. It had been a rental for years, a sort of halfway house for family members. Aunt LaNae had lived there for awhile in addition to a string of cousins and aunts and uncles who moved in, partied, and vanished as easily as they arrived, leaving its screen door clapping in the breeze. Dogs had at some point taken over the house and their feces was caked into the cobalt-blue carpeting upstairs. Mice skittered across the floor. The backyard was a weed-choked junkyard with a sagging dog run, a tipped-over snowmobile, strewn oil cans and beer bottles.

My parents would restore it. In their spare time.

I looked forward to the move. As bad as it was, the Gray House was at least a house, and could, perhaps, even be called a home. After all, it had a yard.

But as I would soon learn, it was a house that required apologies. My new circle of friends, the Monsanto-Mormon friends, would say, "You *live* here?"

"We're renovating it," I would say miserably.

It seems now that we had been in the business of renovation for years, although we never really got to see the end product of our refurbishing.

Perhaps, though, *we* were the end product.

A year passed. And business never picked up. It remained sluggish. It was a slouching economy, and it was all my parents could do to keep the doors open and the bills paid. Not surprisingly the situation rekindled resentments that had never been fully tamped out. Dad, a man haunted by the floodwaters of an impoverished childhood, was a determined if maniacal saver. And this fresh burden chewed away, dollar by dollar, their savings. He took Union calls that were closer to Soda Springs (which meant lower-paying jobs), often driving back and forth from Pocatello to supplement the income, to staunch the flow of money that coursed through that brick fortress. The tens of thousands of dollars he must have watched pour through his fingers.

They rarely spoke to one another. Their conversations were automated and strained, they were porcelain.

When I got home late at night from play rehearsals or a club meeting or from a girl's house, Dad would be sitting in the living room with the lights out and the television on, transfixed, while my mother tossed and turned in the bedroom. On alternate nights, Dad thrashed in bed while my mother sat in the kitchen with the lights off, the orange ember of her cigarette alerting me to her lurking presence.

"What's up?" I'd ask.

"Can't sleep," she'd say, adding a quick redirect: "How was your night?"

Part of renovating the house involved painting the eaves. Scraping the old paint off, priming the gray wood, and painting over the primer. But the old wood drank the primer and required multiple coats. This was my job for the bulk of a summer. I assembled and disassembled a labyrinthine scaffolding apparatus and moved it around the house foot-by-foot. And every day Dad would get home from Pocatello and stop at the house to check on my progress before going to the Enders to begin his work day there. If my progress was not sufficient in his mind—an ever-moving target—we would fight.

One of the worst fights occurred on a bright August afternoon before my junior year in high school. I had a date that night with a Mormon girl named Rosetta. We were going to the movie and I was looking forward to it. I knocked off work early and lounged around the house. When Dad's truck pulled in the driveway, I braced myself for the fight as he walked around the house examining the eaves. And when he stepped inside, he said nothing, only signaled for me to come outside with his finger, as in "come here."

I followed.

"Tell me what you did today?" he asked, framing the argument.

"Some of that old paint on the corner was—"

"I didn't ask for excuses. Now tell me what *exactly* you got done today while the rest of the world worked."

"I—"

"You what?" He stepped closer.

I looked down at the grass which had turned green and plush since we moved in.

"You what? Huh?"

"I—"

The clap to the side of my head came from nowhere. "*You what?*"

"*Jesus!*" I said, injured, holding my ear which was hot from the strike. "What the hell was that?"

"That was to get your attention."

"What is your problem? All I *do* is this shit. Work on this shit hole of a house. All fucking day. And it's never good enough for you. And it never will be."

The punch to my mouth came faster than the blow that preceded it. And in one move, he had taken me down to the ground. Blood filled my mouth and my lip was numb. I was crying. The thing I hated most. The pain I could take. But the humiliation was different. That I couldn't stand. Feeling that small, that vulnerable. It was more than I could take.

Everything then was more than any of us could take.

As always, Dad felt miserable after our fights once he cooled down. A two-or three-day lull would follow while another layer of conversational strain settled on top of the existing one.

When it got really bad during those days, I told my mother that something had to give. There wasn't room in that house for all three of us. And she would nod and stare off into emptiness. Then she would ash her cigarette and say, "Don't think that I haven't thought about it, Brandon. That if I had to make a choice between my husband and my son, I would choose my son in a heartbeat." Her voice would crack. "But don't ask me to make that choice, because it's not fair." And she would cup her hands to her face and leave the room.

The worse things got at home, the more I buried myself in my school world. I spent precious few moments at home and was only there long enough to eat (if I didn't eat at the café), to shower, or to sleep. But this caused problems, too, because if I came in too late, I risked waking Dad up which was considered the worst of all crimes considering they had to wake up at four in the morning. And because the wooden staircase to my room rose over their bedroom, I woke them often despite the time and care I took crawling the creaking staircase. And very often I was jerked out of bed at four in the morning by a raging man.

"You want to play all night then by God you'll wake when the rest of us do," he'd scream. And both he and my mother would invoke the most ironic—for us—of all parental reprimands: "Contrary to what you might think, this ain't a hotel where you can just come and go as you please, mister."

No. It wasn't a hotel.

39. College

I had decided to go to college, and had expected my parents to foot the bill. I scarcely knew what college was and my grades had seldom seen marks above Cs with the exception of maybe my English classes.

I could not have known the financial demands on my family during that taut period. I might have sensed it the way kids often do, but the real, tangible side of financial strain—the expense column eclipsing the income column—was an abstraction, utterly lost on me.

But I had my demands.

I was going to college.

They were going to pay for it.

I needed to get out.

"You've already lived your life," I yelled. "Your life is over! At least let me live mine!"

"Oh, fuck you," Dad said.

The blow I had leveled, I could see, was huge and unfair, and I wanted to take it back.

"He didn't mean that, Buddy," my mother said.

I hung my head with my arms folded in front of me.

"Why not go to ISU?" My mother suggested, meaning the college in Pocatello. "Go to Vo-tech, Brandon. There's good jobs to be had in Vo-tech. You can live here and commute. See how you like it."

"You don't get it. I want *out*. As far away as I can get. If I don't get out I will *fucking die*."

"Watch your mouth."

"Grandma gets it. Why don't you?"

My grandmother did get it. She supported the idea even if she had her secret doubts about how I might do in college. The argument volleyed back and forth. Why did I just think of college now? College is something you plan for. It takes years of savings. You can't just decide on a whim.

I understood this. But I was desperate and I pleaded. And, besides, I had found a school. A liberal arts college in southern Utah. They had a Shakespeare program. I had not only been acting in plays, gone to competitions, but I had even written a play (or generously borrowed the material from a radio play I had once heard, and spun it as my own). My friend, Heidi, was going to the same school to dance and eventually become a choreographer. I would go with her.

Finally they agreed, and in the end, they said their goodbyes and handed me an envelope with several thousand dollars in travelers' checks. "For tuition and a little extra," my mother had said. Dad, who had resigned himself to the idea, extended his hand: "Good luck, pard."

"Okay. Thanks." I climbed in Heidi's small white pickup brimming with our belongings—my snowboard, trunk, duffel bag, guitar, and the eight or so books I owned—and we pulled out of our driveway and headed south.

I reinvented myself at college. I had joined a fraternity, declared English, not Theatre, as my major, and felt more alive than I had at any other time in my life. I had so many stories to tell when I got home.

But what I found when I returned for Thanksgiving break was a home life more sea-tossed than when I had left it. My mother was distraught. They were closing the Enders. "We just can't do it," she said one day at the kitchen table. "We're broke. Flat broke."

"So what's going to happen to the hotel?"

"Grandma put it up for sale."

My stomach slipped. "What?" The words fired automatically. "She can't. I mean, she just can't."

"What other choice does the woman have, Brandon? The taxes alone are enough to eat her alive. And what other choice do *we* have? We've all done our best."

"But can't she just hang on?"

"Jesus, Brandon, that is all she has done for seventeen years is hang on. That's all any of us has done, is hang on."

And if that wasn't enough of a blow, she delivered another. She took a drag from her cigarette and exhaled. "And there's something else you need to know." She took one more drag, stubbed out the cigarette, and lit another. "I am leaving your dad."

I tried to speak but nothing came out. And then I managed a tepid, "Why?"

"Because," she said. Something had come between them, something that had everything to do with the hotel, and no one, really, could have been surprised that a marriage—strained even under the best circumstances—would buckle under the weight of such a place.

"You just can't *leave*."

"And give me one good reason why not."

"Because what would you do? What would any of us do?" I paused. "It was the hotel," I said. "We were totally trapped there. You know that. It killed Grandpa. It nearly killed Grandma. And besides, he's the only dad I've got."

She nodded her head and started to cry. "I know," she said. "I know."

It was a strange turn of events, and surprising, too, in just how easily I had protested the sale of the hotel only to turn around and blame the place for this kind of collateral damage. But a place can be a complicated thing.

My parents worked through their differences and announced that they would stay together about the same time my grandmother announced that she had sold the Enders Hotel, Café, and Bar.

When William and Theodore Enders broke ground in 1917, they paid $16,000.

When my grandparents bought it in early 1975, they paid $250,000.

She sold it in 1992 for $85,000.

When I pressed her on this once, she put up her hands as if blocking my words and said, "Damn it, Brandon. I had to do what I had to do. It was going to kill me."

40. Enders

After that, my parents seemed like new people. They focused solely on renovating the Gray House. They put up white siding and gray shutters and covered the very eaves I had spent an entire summer scraping, sanding, priming, and painting. Dad laughs about it still. "Yeah. I feel bad about that, pard. I didn't know we were going to put a new roof on and that the eaves would be covered, too."

It's a long running joke in the family. The overdone renovation.

For years every time I returned home to visit I would drive by the Enders Hotel slowly and stare into its windows hoping to see, to see what, exactly? To see us again? To find some immutable truth? To be reassured that a place is just a place, and that people come out the other side changed somehow? That it all ends eventually? Even bricks that so often outlive their foundries and their masons, slip out of their plumb line? That the mortar crumbles and that all we are left with are the stories? That in the end, it was our suitcases left behind to float in the green waters of forgetting? Or that for seventeen years we gave more than any family should be asked to give for a place?

Or perhaps this: that we were all of us enders in our own ways, not so different from those we boarded, those we fed, those who drank on our stools, who died in our parking lot, or on our floor; or those who were beaten on our stairs, or those who tried to find solace within our walls. Perhaps they came to us because they recognized us, and we saw in them some part of ourselves. No. We weren't so different after all.

We were all of us enders, all of us just people in the pattern.

Epilogue

It is July 2006 and I am driving a teeth-clattering dirt road in one of the most barren and remote stretches of southeastern Idaho. The drive, I know, will take me better than two hours as my car growls through ruts, buttonhook turns, and rain-washed gullies. This is an eighty-some-odd mile ribbon of stone-knuckled trail called the Bone Road. Mine is the only car for miles in any direction. I have just learned only hours earlier, and by complete accident, that my father, Jerrold Imeson—a man I have known only by name, a man I have never met, never seen—is dead. That he in fact died nearly ten years ago: heart failure. He was forty-four. And then moments later, I learned that *his* father, Jim, another man I have never met, never seen, had died at forty-six: cancer. And the final blow: *his* father, Jim Sr., died at forty-five of unknown causes. I am thirty-three and driving the long way back to visit the Enders Hotel. I am haunted. I resist the simple math and what the mortality rates of these strangers with whom I share blood suggest.

I resist the probabilities and drive like a madman, throwing the car sidelong into hard, washboard turns, gunning it over steep rocky rises. I mash the accelerator to the floor and grip the wheel.

Sweat slides down my back as sunlight burns white against the windshield. It is ninety degrees. A buckled plain of sagebrush and cheatgrass splattered with cow shit trails off into the hazy smudge of summer sky. Not even a single juniper breaks the sight-line on this tumbling world. The windows are down and I grind the dust in my clenched teeth. A crumpled photocopy of my father's obituary floats and spins kite-like in the seat next to me.

It has been a long drive from the northern part of the state where I teach at the University of Idaho. My wife and two children are with her family for the weekend just over the border in Wyoming. "I have to figure some things out," I tell my wife on the phone after I learned about my father.

I spot a dead coyote along the road. At first I think it's a dog, but I stop and take a closer look. Its grayish coat and arrowed snout say coyote. Its head is nearly severed from the rest of the body, cocked and pointed over its back. Its jaws scissored, lips pulled back, teeth exposed. It was snarling when it died, I think, moments after it had been hit along this road. This is the first coyote I have seen up close, and its fur is matted and its flesh picked over by turkey vultures, no doubt. Its gray entrails balloon from the whitish stomach. Carrion, I think and climb back into the car.

I camp one night along the Bone Road, at the edge of the Blackfoot Reservoir. The water is blue and smooth like it has been grabbed at the shores and pulled taut. Two pelicans glide over the water in front of me, their reflections clear on the water. The carcass of a large carp is decomposing ten feet from my tent. Its eye looks like a rare medallion. I build a fire out of sagebrush and watch a toad hop toward the water's edge. Though I know I shouldn't, I drink an entire bottle of wine and rock back and forth on a log before the crackling fire. Tomorrow I will go back to the Enders Hotel one last time.

In 2000, Rex Maughan, a Soda Springs native who made his fortune in the aloe business, bought the Enders from Louise Collard, the person to whom my grandmother had sold it nine years earlier. During those years, the basement filled with swamp-green water, knee deep, where the flotsam of eighty-three years of stories floated in the form of letters, papers, playing cards, and photographs mottled with mold. Louise closed off both of the upper floors of the hotel within six months of owning it, within six months of trying to pay the heating bills. Soon after, it was condemned. But now it's a museum, gift shop, and B&B. Fully restored to its 1917 floor plan. A million dollar renovation. New oak, marble, and brass everywhere. They spared no expense.

I look like hell. I have just come off the Bone Road and my head is pounding from the wine. I am road-beaten with bloodshot eyes as I wander around the lobby. I walk past the showcases in the museum and take notice of the relics of my past, entombed behind glass. Other items stand out in the open, guarded, though, by note cards that read DO NOT TOUCH: the old adding machine with its green, white, black, and red keys round as buttons, brilliant like candies; the old barber chair; brass lamps; baroque paintings; the flat green tins of Lucky Strikes; empty whisky bottles choked with rotting corks, and everything and on and on.

I find none of our stories in the glass hutches. I stare at the museum of my life and nothing in any of the displays suggests I had ever been there. We are not mentioned at all. Our family's story has been omitted from this rendition.

Nor does the museum speak to all those people who passed through this place. No word of the medicinally scented quarters of Maya. Or the lumpy beds that once held a boxing champion, an ex-con, a murderer, a poor family bound for what they called home, or any of the faces who passed between. The museum says nothing at all about the Enders family themselves, about the brothers who shared an idea, raised the money, and hauled in the brick.

I step into the ballroom and look around. It is surreal. I have been in here since the renovation, but it gets more, not less, surreal each time back. I rock my heels on the wood floor and then look up into the skylight. This used to be my bedroom. Now it is a ballroom. I laugh. Large picture windows stare out onto the geyser. It has just erupted and a pack of tourists are dispersing. My old stone clubhouse still stands at the base of the geyser though it is boarded up and padlocked shut. The city now owns it.

I step from the ballroom back into the lobby which is lined with high-back leather rockers. The telephone switchboard that I used to play with has been exhumed and cleaned up. I look around and exhale. I am tired. And I am at once at ease and bereft. I am the only one in my family to have visited the Enders Hotel since the restoration. They want nothing to do with the place. I feel differently of course because it was my home.

I push through the lobby doors and step outside on to the hot sidewalk. The sky is orange from a slag pour and I turn around to catch my reflection in the lobby window. It appears as if I am standing in the Enders Hotel, staring back at myself in a face-off: me and my ghost.

Winners of the River Teeth Literary Nonfiction Prize

Five Shades of Shadow
Tracy Daugherty

The Untouched Minutes
Donald Morrill

Where the Trail Grows Faint:
A Year in the Life of a Therapy Dog Team
Lynne Hugo

The World Before Mirrors
Joan Connor

House of Good Hope:
A Promise for a Broken City
Michael Downs

The Enders Hotel: A Memoir
Brandon R. Schrand

UNIVERSITY OF NEBRASKA PRESS